北京高等教育精品教材
BEIJING GAODENG JIAOYU JINGPIN JIAOCAI

新世纪应用英语教程 2

学生用书

苏联波　赵建礼　主编

北京大学出版社
PEKING UNIVERSITY PRESS

图书在版编目(CIP)数据

新世纪应用英语教程(2)学生用书 / 苏联波,赵建礼主编. —北京:北京大学出版社,2007.2
 (全国高职高专公共英语教材)
 ISBN 978-7-301-10354-8

Ⅰ.新… Ⅱ.①苏…②赵… Ⅲ.英语-高等学校:技术学校-教学参考资料 Ⅳ.H31

中国版本图书馆 CIP 数据核字(2005)第 147190 号

书　　　名:	新世纪应用英语教程(2)(学生用书)
著作责任者:	苏联波　赵建礼　主编
责任编辑:	刘　爽
标准书号:	ISBN 978-7-301-10354-8/H·1631
出版发行:	北京大学出版社
地　　　址:	北京市海淀区成府路 205 号　100871
网　　　址:	http://www.pup.cn
电　　　话:	邮购部 62752015　发行部 62750672　编辑部 62755217　出版部 62754962
电子邮箱:	zbing@pup.pku.edu.cn
印　刷　者:	北京大学印刷厂
经　销　者:	新华书店
	787毫米×1092毫米　16 开本　14.75 印张　300 千字
	2007 年 2 月第 1 版　2012 年 8 月第 14 次印刷
定　　　价:	24.80 元(附赠光盘)

未经许可,不得以任何方式复制或抄袭本书之部分或全部内容。

版权所有,侵权必究　举报电话:010-62752024
　　　　　　　　　　　 电子邮箱:fd@pup.pku.edu.cn

主　编　苏联波　赵建礼
副主编　柴　明　黎富玉　车炳银　杨　远

编　委（以姓氏笔画顺序排名）
　　　王昭飞　车炳银　尹山鹰　付　静　刘远志
　　　刘维一　阳　勇　苏联波　李　玲　李晓华
　　　邹雪茜　周　成　赵建礼　柴　明　曾　尼
　　　谢　敏　廖建英　黎富玉

前　　言

　　《全国高职高专公共英语教材》是为进一步落实国家《2003—2007年教育振兴行动计划》，在广泛调研的基础上依据教育部《高职高专教育英语课程教学基本要求》(以下简称《基本要求》)特为全国高职高专非英语专业学生编写的一套公共英语教材，并被列入"十一五"国家重点出版规划项目《面向新世纪的立体化网络化英语学科建设丛书》。本套教材取材丰富，题材多样，贴近生活，时代感强，是一套集应用性、实用性、趣味性和文化性为一体的特色英语教科书。为方便学生学习和教学安排，本教材分为两大体系：《新世纪应用英语教程》(着重于读、写、译)和《新世纪交际英语教程》(着重于视、听、说)。这两大体系既相照应又相包容，不仅使听、说、读、写、译五大语言基本技能训练得到有效的整合，并科学地贯穿于英语教学的全过程，而且还从不同的角度为学生的语言学习提供生动多元的文化氛围和真实丰富的语言环境，从而使语言学习、语言实践、语言应用以及文化体验有机结合，十分有利于学生语言应用能力的培养与提高。

　　本教材为《新世纪应用英语教程》，其特色主要体现在以下几个方面：

　　1. **布局科学合理，能很好地满足《基本要求》关于分级教学、分级指导之需要。**全套书共分三册，第一、二册为B级(过渡级)要求，适用于入学时英语水平较低的学生，通过学习应认知2500个英语词汇；学完第三册书达到A级(标准级)要求，应认知3400个英语词汇，词汇覆盖率达到98%；在体例编排上，通过对构成本教材主体的课文主题、语法项目、实用英语等项目的科学安排，使本教材第一、二册在相对独立而自成体系的同时与第三册形成有机联系，以方便老师的教学和学生对本教材的使用。

　　2. **针对性强，很好地体现了《基本要求》的精神。**全书各项目安排均紧密围绕培养学生具有与日后职业生涯所必需的英语交际能力这一中心来进行，其中"实用英语"教学项目的安排与选材便是一大亮点，其主要内容均是极具实用性的应用文，如各种事务信函、广告、卡片、条据、产品介绍、求职简历等。

　　3. **加强"双基"教学，突出语言实践。**坚持"应用为主、够用为度、学以致用、触类旁通"的方针，以实践为主线，理论知识点到为止。在精读课文、阅读材料、语法项目、实用英语等的教学安排上均结合学生实际，在加强学生基础知识训练的同时十分注重学生读、写、译等基础技能的训练。

　　4. **注重学生自我发展能力的培养。**为此，本教程分别在精读课文和阅读材料前安排了"导学"和"导读"。这样做既方便学生课前学习，又有助于他们逐渐养成自学的习惯，从而不断增强他们这方面的能力。

　　5. **强调寓教于乐和学生文化素养的提高。**"英语沙龙"便是特意为此而设立，主要内容有名人名言、谚语、短诗、幽默小品等易于上口、便于记忆而又不失风趣与教育意义的韵文。

6. 配备多媒体网络系统和电子课件。 提供图文、声音、视频等传统教程难以提供的多方位的学习资料；提供学生的个性化学习平台；提供教学内容的持续更新和动态扩展。

《新世纪应用英语教程》从教学实际出发，将传统教科书的每册10个单元改为8个单元，每个单元由五大部分组成。单元中的各组成部分不仅功能突出、特色鲜明，而且都服务于培养学生应用能力这一中心，使整个单元形成一个有机的整体，具体如下：

Part 1 课文(Text)——此为精读课文，主要为学生打好语言基础。

Part 2 语法(Grammar)——按语法项目进行较系统的专项练习，为学生语言技能的培养打基础。

Part 3 阅读(Reading)——阅读材料内容与课文(Text)的主题相关，强调知识性与趣味性。主要目的是在扩大学生词汇量的同时，开阔学生视野，加强学生阅读能力。

Part 4 实用英语 (Practical English)——结合高职高专学生今后职业生涯中应用英语的实际，并根据《基本要求》中有关语言交际能力的具体要求，着重安排实用性应用文章，如信函、广告、产品介绍、个人简历等。

Part 5 英语沙龙(English Salon)——目的是寓教于乐，在提高学生文化素质的同时以潜移默化的方式加深学生对英语语言的理解。着重安排：名人名言、谚语、短诗、幽默小品文等易于上口、便于记忆、又不失幽默与教育意义的韵文。

本系列教材具有高品位和权威性，由北京大学享受两院院士级待遇的文科资深教授胡壮麟先生担任总顾问，北京大学英语系教授孙亦丽先生担任总主编，北京交通大学、重庆大学、成都大学等教学科研第一线的骨干教师参与编写工作。

本教材在编写过程中得到诸多老师和同仁的关心、指导和帮助，我们对此表示衷心感谢。除署名作者外，本书承外籍教授 Paul Crutcher 审阅并提出宝贵修改意见，教师黄曦、张岚和宋英等也参与了本教材的编写工作，在此一并表示感谢。但限于作者水平，加之时间紧促，如有不当之处，恳请各位读者及专家批评指正。

2005 年 10 月

Unit One 1

Part I	Text	1
Part II	Grammar	13
Part III	Reading Practice	17
Part IV	Practical English	22
Part V	English Salon	25

Unit Two 26

Part I	Text	26
Part II	Grammar	36
Part III	Reading Practice	41
Part IV	Practical English	45
Part V	English Salon	49

Unit Three 50

Part I	Text	50
Part II	Grammar	62
Part III	Reading Practice	66
Part IV	Practical English	72
Part V	English Salon	77

Unit Four 78

Part I	Text	78
Part II	Grammar	88
Part III	Reading Practice	92
Part IV	Practical English	96
Part V	English Salon	101

Unit Five 102

Part I	Text	102
Part II	Grammar	114
Part III	Reading Practice	117
Part IV	Practical English	122
Part V	English Salon	128

Unit Six 129

Part I	Text	129
Part II	Grammar	141
Part III	Reading Practice	145
Part IV	Practical English	150
Part V	English Salon	154

Unit Seven 156

Part I	Text	156
Part II	Grammar	167
Part III	Reading Practice	172
Part IV	Practical English	177
Part V	English Salon	181

Unit Eight 183

Part I	Text	183
Part II	Grammar	193
Part III	Reading Practice	197
Part IV	Practical English	201
Part V	English Salon	206

Vocabulary 207

Unit One

Part I TEXT

Guide to Text-Learning

1. Words and Expressions Related to the Topic

degree	学位
bachelor	文理学士
master	硕士
doctor	博士
undergraduate	大学生
graduate	研究生
tuition	学费
tutor	（大学）指导教师，助教
extracurricular	课外的
loan	贷款
financial aid	财政援助

2. Grammatical Structures to Learn

(1) The university **was named** after a Puritan religious leader, John Harvard.
学校以一位清教徒领袖约翰·哈佛的名字命名。

(2) It has been extended into a university of the first rank, **free from** all religious control.
后来它完全摆脱了宗教的控制，逐渐发展成为一流的高等学府。

(3) Students find activities in dance, drama, journalism, music, religion, visual arts, and **a variety of** other special interest areas.
学生们可以参加舞蹈、戏剧、新闻、音乐、宗教、视觉艺术以及各种各样其他的兴趣活动。

1

> **Warming-Up Questions:**
> 1. Can you name out the first ten top universities in the world?
> 2. What is the difference between Harvard University and Harvard College?
> 3. Say something about Harvard according to your knowledge.

Harvard

1 Harvard University, the oldest university in America, began in 1636 in Massachusetts, near Boston. The university was named after a Puritan religious leader, John Harvard, who by the **heritage** of his library and small **fortune** helped to **launch** the **institution** in 1638; it was originally intended for the training of youths for the Puritan ministry, but it has been extended into a university of the first **rank**, free from all religious control. Many famous people studied at Harvard. Seven presidents of the United States were graduates of Harvard. Its faculty have produced more than 40 Nobel Prizes.

2 The University has grown from nine students with a single master to an **enrollment** of more than 18,000 degree **candidates**, including undergraduates and students in 10 **principal academic** units. An additional 13,000 students have enrolled in one or more courses in the Harvard Extension School. More than 3,000 are from outside the United States. Most of the foreign students are from Asia or Europe. Most are studying for graduate degrees.

3 Many years ago, Harvard students were all white men. Most of them were from rich families

---

heritage /ˈheritidʒ/ n.
something that is passed down from preceding generations
遗产;传统

fortune /ˈfɔːtʃən/ n.
wealth
大量财产;财富

launch /lɔːntʃ/ v.
set going; initiate
发动;开始

institution /ˌinstiˈtjuːʃən/ n.
an established organization or foundation, especially one dedicated to education, public service, or culture
(教育或文化)机构

rank /ræŋk/ n.
a relative position or degree of value in a graded group
顺序,次序

enrollment /inˈrəulmənt/ v.
the act or process of enrolling
注册,登记

candidate /ˈkændidit/ n.
a person taking an examination
应试者

principal /ˈprinsəpəl/ adj.
chief
重要的,首要的

academic /ˌækəˈdemik/ adj.
relating to scholarly performance
有关学术的

from northeastern states. That has changed. At present, about thirty-three percent of the first-year students at Harvard are from **minority** groups. These include African Americans, Asian Americans and Hispanic Americans. Almost fifty percent of first-year students are women. Today, most Harvard students are not rich,

although it is very **costly** to study there. It costs more than forty thousand dollars for one year for tuition, room, food and personal expenses. Most of the students at Harvard have loans, financial aid or jobs that help pay for their education.

4   Many experts consider Harvard to be the best university in the United States. It is very difficult to be accepted to study there. More than 19,000 high school students applied to attend Harvard as undergraduates in 2002. About 1,600 of them began studying there in September.

5   Harvard University includes Harvard College and the following graduate schools: the Graduate School of Arts and Sciences, the Business School, the Design School, the **Divinity** School, the School of Education, the John F. Kennedy School of Government, the Law School, and the Schools of **Dental** Medicine, Medicine, and Public Health. In 1879, Harvard opened a college for women. It was called Radcliffe College. Its medical college and law school are among the best in the country.

6   Harvard is located in Cambridge, a city on the banks of the Charles River, across from Boston. There are many shops, bookstores, and restaurants. Tourists go to Harvard Square to see the famous campus, shops, and buy Harvard T-shirts. Both Boston and Cambridge enjoy a history of tradition, as **illustrated** by their concert halls, libraries and bookstores, museums, theaters, coffeehouses, shops,

> **minority** /mai'nɔriti/ *n.*
> a racial, religious, political, national, or other group regarded as different from the larger group of which it is part
> 少数
>
> **costly** /'kɔstli/ *adj.*
> expensive
> 昂贵的
>
> **divinity** /di'viniti/ *n.*
> theology
> 神学
>
> **dental** /'dentl/ *adj.*
> of, relating to, or intended for dentistry
> 牙科的
>
> **illustrate** /'iləstrieit/ *v.*
> clarify, as by use of examples or comparisons
> 说明

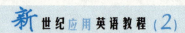

and playgrounds. The cultural and recreational opportunities are countless and easily accessible. Beaches and mountains are both conveniently near.

7   The residential plan for undergraduate students is an **essential** part of the Harvard experience. Every student is **assured** a place in College housing for four years. Freshmen live in one of the several **dormitories** in Harvard Yard, the oldest and most central part of the campus. At the end of the freshman year, students move into residential houses in which they will live for the rest part of their undergraduate **careers**. The house system provides a smaller community for students within the larger University environment. Each house has a resident senior **faculty** member who is called the master, a senior tutor or dean, a tutorial **staff**, a library, and dining **facilities**. All houses are coeducational, and much of the social, athletic, extracurricular, and academic life centers on the house.

8   Harvard offers more than 250 student organizations. Students find activities in dance, **drama**, **journalism**, music, religion, **visual** arts, and a variety of other special interest areas.

(629 Words)

---

essential /i'senʃəl/ *adj.*
basic or indispensable; necessary
基本的,必须的

assure /ə'ʃuə/ *v.*
cause to feel sure
使确信

dormitory /'dɔ:mitri/ *n.*
a building for housing a number of persons, as at a school
宿舍

career /kə'riə/ *n.*
the general course of one's working life
生涯,经历

faculty /'fækəlti/ *n.*
a body of teachers
全体教师

staff /stɑ:f/ *n.*
the personnel who carry out a specific enterprise
全体雇员

facility /fə'siliti/ *n.*
sth created to serve a particular function
设备

drama /'drɑ:mə/ *n.*
theatrical plays of a particular kind or period
戏剧

journalism /'dʒɜ:nlizəm/ *n.*
collecting, writing, editing, and presentation of news or news articles in newspapers and magazines and in radio and television broadcasts
新闻报道

visual /'vizjuəl/ *adj.*
of or relating to the sense of sight
视力的,视觉的

Useful Phrases

name after	give the same name as	以……命名
extend (from)... into...	be or become long, large, or comprehensive	扩大;使变得……
(be) free from	not affected or restricted by	解除;没有……的
at present	at the present time; right now	现在,马上
pay for	give money to in return for...	支付
be located in/at	be placed at a certain location	位于……
a variety of	a number or collection of varied things	各种各样的

Proper Names

Harvard University	哈佛大学
Massachusetts	马萨诸塞州
Boston	波士顿
Cambridge	剑桥
Puritan	清教徒(的)
African American	非裔美国人
Asian American	亚裔美国人
Hispanic American	西班牙裔美国人
Harvard College	哈佛学院
Radcliffe College	拉德克利夫学院
Nobel Prize	诺贝尔奖

1. ... but it has been extended into a university of the first rank, free from all religious control. ……后来它完全摆脱了宗教的控制,逐渐发展成为一流的高等学府。

   free from all religious control 为形容词短语,用作伴随状语。

2. The University has grown from nine students with a single master to an enrollment of more than 18,000 degree candidates, including undergraduates and students in 10 principal academic units. 哈佛当初只有一名教师,招收了九名学生;如今在校学生人数已达一万八千多名,包括本科生和在十个研究生院学习的研究生。

   grow from... to/into... "由……长成……;由……发展成为……"例如:
   It has grown from a rural village to a modern town. 这地方已由一个小乡村发展成为一个现代化的城镇。

   include v. take in as a part, an element, or a member "包括"。例如:
   Our ten-day tour included a visit to Stratford. 我们的十日游还包括到斯特拉特福德市的参观。

   该词常用现在分词引起一个解释性短语。例如:
   At least 80 persons were injured, including five policemen. 至少有80人受伤,包括五名警察。

3. Both Boston and Cambridge enjoy a history of tradition, as illustrated by their concert halls, libraries and bookstores, museums, theaters, coffeehouses, shops, and playgrounds. 波士顿和剑桥都有着悠久的历史,它们的音乐厅、图书馆、书店、博物馆、剧院、咖啡屋、商店和运动场无一不展示着这一特色。

   as illustrated... 可看成是一个省略句,原句为: as is illustrated..., 用作非限制性定语从句。

4. All houses are coeducational, and much of the social, athletic, extracurricular, and academic life centers on the house. 所有的会馆都是男女生混合的,学生们的社交、体育、课外活动以及学习生活都是

以会馆为中心。

center *vi.* have a central theme or concern; be focused "具有中心主题或关注,聚焦"。例如:

Her novels center on the problems of adolescence. 她的小说以青少年问题为中心。

Reading Aloud and Memorizing the Following

I. Read the following paragraph taken from the text until you learn it by heart.

The residential plan for undergraduate students is an essential part of the Harvard experience. Every student is assured a place in College housing for four years. Freshmen live in one of the several dormitories in Harvard Yard, the oldest and most central part of the campus. At the end of the freshman year, students move into residential houses in which they will live for the rest part of their undergraduate careers. The house system provides a smaller community for students within the larger University environment. Each house has a resident senior faculty member who is called the master, a senior tutor or dean, a tutorial staff, a library, and dining facilities. All houses are coeducational, and much of the social, athletic, extracurricular, and academic life centers on the house.

Comprehension of the Text

II. Choose the best answer to each of the following questions according to the passage.

1. Why did the university change its name to Harvard?
   A. Somebody gave the university a lot of money.
   B. John Harvard was the first teacher.
   C. A priest told them to change the name.
   D. John Harvard gave the university many things.

2. In 1638, _____.

   A. John Harvard died

   B. a US president visited Harvard

   C. the school was very big

   D. the business school was important

3. Radcliffe College _____.

   A. was started by John Harvard

   B. enrolled female students only

   C. was Harvard's first school

   D. opened 50 years ago

4. About _____ of the applicants for Harvard can be admitted into college every year.

   A. more than 10 percent

   B. less than 10 percent

   C. more than 20 percent

   D. less than 20 percent

5. Which of the statement is true?

   A. Harvard only has students from America.

   B. There are very few different classes at Harvard.

   C. The university was always called Harvard.

   D. Harvard was America's first university.

III. Answer the following questions with the information you've got from the text.

1. What was the original purpose of the foundation of Harvard University?　(Para. 1)
2. How can you describe Harvard when it was just launched?　(Para. 2)
3. What do you know about graduate schools of Harvard?　(Para. 5)
4. Freshmen of Harvard are required to live on campus, aren't they?　(Para. 7)
5. Can students make films by themselves according to the passage?　(Para. 8)

Vocabulary

IV. Spell out the words with the help of the given definitions and the first letters.

1. give a name to (n _____)

2. first or earliest (o _____)
3. one who has received an academic degree or diploma (g _____)
4. a college or university student who has not yet received a bachelor's degree (u _____)
5. a complete body of prescribed studies constituting a curriculum (c _____)
6. fee for instruction, especially at a formal institution of learning (t _____)
7. an artificial embankment (b _____)
8. station or situate (l _____)
9. supply (p _____)
10. the chief executive of a republic (p _____)

V. Fill in the blanks with the words given below. Change the form where necessary.

| academy | education | enroll | fortune | illustrate |
| include | intend | pay | produce | resident |

1. The old lady is _____ enough to have very good health.
2. During my _____ trip to Beijing next month I'd like to have a chance to enjoy some Peking operas.
3. _____ of computers has increased double in the last few weeks.
4. The class has a(n) _____ of 47 students.
5. Peking University is a famous _____ institution.
6. _____ may be made in any of the following ways, by cash, by cheque, or by credit card.
7. He _____ a large number of funny stories in the speech.
8. The scientist cited vivid instances in _____ of his theory.
9. Their _____ building is located next to the park.
10. It was really a(n) _____ film.

VI. Fill in the blanks with proper prepositions or adverbs.
1. The wet weather extended _____ September.
2. The international corporation paid $500,000 _____ the firm.
3. They named the child _____ both grandparents.
4. What I have said does not apply _____ you.

5. Their factory is located _____ the foot of the mountain.
6. She provides _____ her family by working in a hospital.
7. He is on holiday _____ present.
8. They tried to center the discussion _____ the main issues.
9. The old lady is never free _____ pain.
10. He has grown _____ a real man.

Structure

VII. Rewrite the following sentences after the models.

Model 1   The university **was given a name of** a Puritan religious leader, John Harvard.

The university **was named** after a Puritan religious leader, John Harvard.

1. They gave their child the name Janet.
2. Did you ever hear of a painter whose name was Raphael?
3. We shall call this ship Princess Alice.
4. The girl was called Julia—after her mother.
5. What will you call the baby?

Model 2   Students find activities in dance, drama, journalism, music, religion, visual arts, and **various kinds of** other special interest areas.

Students find activities in dance, drama, journalism, music, religion, visual arts, and **a variety of** other special interest areas.

1. Susan came home from work and brought all kinds of snacks.
2. He didn't come for many different reasons.
3. She made the children glad by all kinds of means.
4. He was interested in many things, which made him an agreeable companion.
5. The Smithsonian Institution has a wide range of objects on display.

VIII. Study the model and translate the following sentences into English, by using the phrase "(be) free from."

Model: It has been extended into a university of the first rank, **free from** all religious control.

1. 他希望能过上一种完全无忧无虑的生活。
2. 我服用了三片阿司匹林,这样可以止痛半个小时。
3. 那位老人一直痛苦不堪。
4. 桌上放一块布以免把桌面弄脏。
5. 他的作文没有语法错误。

Translation

IX. Translate the following sentences into Chinese.

1. Harvard University, the oldest university in America, began in 1636 in Massachusetts, near Boston.

2. Today, most Harvard students are not rich, although it is very costly to study there.

3. Harvard University includes Harvard College and the following graduate schools.

4. Harvard is located in Cambridge, a city on the banks of the Charles River, across from Boston.

5. The residential plan for undergraduate students is an essential part of the Harvard experience.

X. Translate the following sentences into English using the words or phrases in the brackets.

1. 那是我国历史上代价最大的战争。(costly)

2. 博物馆就在我们学校旁边。(locate)

3. 他花三美元买了一个汉堡包。(pay for)

4. 现在我们住在北京。(at present)

5. 这儿的所有人都患了流感,包括我在内。(include)

Part II Grammar

Tenses（时态）（一、二）

作谓语的动词用来表示动作(情况)发生时间的各种形式称为时态。在英语中,不同时间发生的动作,要用不同形式的动词来表示。如:

He came yesterday.

He will come tomorrow.

英语共有 16 个时态,以动词 do 为例,列表如下:

一般现在时 do(es)	现在进行时 am/is/are doing	现在完成时 have/has done	现在完成进行时 have/has been doing
一般过去时 did	过去进行时 was/were doing	过去完成时 had done	过去完成进行时 had been doing
一般将来时 shall/will do	将来进行时 shall/will be doing	将来完成时 shall/will have done	将来完成进行时 shall/will have been doing
一般过去将来时 should/would do	过去将来进行时 should/would be doing	过去将来完成时 should/would have done	过去将来完成进行时 should/would have been doing

最常用的时态有五个,即一般现在时、现在进行时、现在完成时、一般过去时和一般将来时,此外,一般过去将来时、过去进行时和过去完成时也较常用。

时态(一)一般时 (Simple Tenses)

一般时态用来表示一般性或习惯性的行为或状态。

1. 一般现在时 (Simple Present Tense)

表示现在经常发生或习惯性的动作,动词用原形,主语是第三人称单数时动词原形后加 s 或 es 形式。常与下列时间状语连用: every..., sometimes, always, never, often, usually 等。例如:

I usually get up at 6:30.

还可用以表示客观真理、客观存在、科学事实。

The earth moves around the sun.

2. 一般过去时 (Simple Past Tense)

表示在确定的过去时间里所发生的动作或存在的状态，动词用过去式形式。常用的时间状语有：yesterday, last week, an hour ago, the other day, in 1967 等。

He arrived in Beijing last night.

还可表示在过去一段时间内，经常性或习惯性的动作。

They lived in the country then.

3. 一般将来时 (Simple Future Tense)

表示将来某个特定时间将要发生的动作或存在的状态，由"shall/will + 动词原形"构成。shall 用于第一人称，在美国英语中常被 will 所代替。will 在陈述句中用于各人称，在征求意见时常用于第二人称。例如：

I shall watch a football match on TV this evening.

Will you be home at seven this evening?

4. 一般过去将来时 (Simple Past Future Tense)

一般过去将来时的出发点是过去，即从过去某一时刻看以后要发生的动作或状态。由"should/would + 动词原形"构成。

He asked me yesterday when I should leave for Paris.

昨天他问我什么时候动身去巴黎。

They wanted to know how they would finish the homework earlier.

他们想知道怎样才能早一点儿完成家庭作业。

时态(二)进行时 (Progressive Tenses)

进行时态用来表示行为的延续，即在某一时间或某段时间正在进行的动作。

1. 现在进行时 (Present Progressive Tense)

表示现在(指说话人说话时)正在发生的动作，由 is/am/are+V.ing 构成。常用的时间状语：now, at the(this) moment... 例如：

I'm waiting for my boy friend.
He is not playing toys.
What are you doing now?

2. 过去进行时 (Past Progressive Tense)

表示过去某一时间或一段时间正在发生的动作，由 was/were+V.ing 构成。例如：

I was doing my homework at that time.
He was not sleeping at 11 o'clock last night.
What were you doing at that moment?

Exercises

I. Fill in the blanks with the proper forms of the verbs given in the brackets.

1. Yesterday I _____ (think) that you were not in Beijing.
2. Alice usually _____ (sit) in the front of the classroom, but she _____ (sit) at the back this morning.
3. He _____ (tell) the news to us three days ago.
4. He _____ (begin) to teach Chinese in 1990.
5. She would not telephone me if she _____ (have) no time.
6. If their house _____ (be) not like ours, what _____ (do) it look like?
7. My brother _____ (fall) while he _____ (ride) his bicycle and hurt himself.
8. On television last night the newscaster announced that the leader _____ (arrive) on Saturday.
9. My aunt _____ (come) to see us, she _____ (be) here soon.
10. The little child does not even know that the moon _____ (move) around the earth.

II. Complete each of the following sentences with the most appropriate word or words from the four choices marked A, B, C and D.

1. He _____ his leg as he _____ in a football match.
   A. broke/played
   B. was breaking/was playing
   C. broke/was playing
   D. was breaking/played

2. —My father will be here tomorrow.
   —I thought that he _____ this morning.
   A. was coming
   B. is coming
   C. will come
   D. comes

3. How can you _____ if you are not _____?
   A. listening/hearing
   B. hear/listening
   C. be listening/heard
   D. be hearing/listening to

4. The girl even won't have her lunch before she _____ her homework.
   A. will finish
   B. is finishing
   C. was finishing
   D. finishes

5. The old scientist _____ to do more for the country.
   A. is wishing
   B. was wishing
   C. wishes
   D. wish

6. He told us that he would begin the dictation when we _____ ready.
   A. will be
   B. would be
   C. were
   D. are

7. They _____ the trip until the rain stopped.
   A. continued
   B. didn't continue
   C. don't continue
   D. would continue

8. The local peasants gave the soldiers clothes and food without which they _____ of hunger and cold.
   A. would die
   B. will die
   C. would be dead
   D. would have died

9. It was not until then that I came to know that the earth _____ around the sun.
   A. moved
   B. has moved
   C. will move
   D. moves

10. When all those present _____ he began his lecture.
    A. sit
    B. set
    C. were seated
    D. seated

Part III Reading Practice

Guide to Reading

1. Words and Expressions to Learn

transform	v.	转换,改变
model	n.	样式,模式
recruit	v.	补充;征募
celebrate	v.	庆祝;赞美;举行
stress	n.	重点,着重,强调
basic	n.&adj.	基础;基本的
comprise	v.	包含,由……组成
personnel	n.	人员,职员
various	adj.	各种各样的,多样的
fundamental	adj.&n.	基础的;基本原则,基本原理
pure	adj.	纯的,纯洁的;完美的
aim	n.	目标,目的
strive	v.	努力,奋斗
Imperial Capital University		京师大学堂
National Peking University		国立北京大学
anti-feudal		反封建的
anti-imperialist		反帝国主义的
anti-Japanese		抗日的

2. Pre-Reading Questions

(1) Do you know when Peking University celebrated her 100 anniversary?
(2) Who was the first president of Peking University?

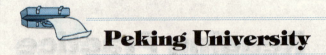

Peking University

1   Peking University was established in Beijing in December 1898 and was originally known as the Imperial Capital University. In 1912, following the Xinhai Revolution, the Imperial Capital University was renamed the National Peking University.

2   The famous scholar Cai Yuanpei was appointed president on January 4, 1917 and helped transform the university into the country's largest institution of higher learning, with 14  departments and an enrollment of more than 2,000 students. Cai, inspired by the German model of academic freedom, recruited an intellectually **diverse** (*adj.* 不同的) faculty that included Hu Shi, Chen Duxiu, and Lu Xun. The anti-imperialist and anti-feudal May 4th Movement in 1919 is the most important moment in the history of Peking University. In some ways, this marks the beginning of the modern age of Chinese history. In order to carry on the revolutionary **tradition** (*n.* 传统) of the May 4th Movement, the university decided, after the new China was founded, that the 4th of May be set as the date on which to celebrate the **anniversary** (*n.* 周年纪念) of the founding of the university. It's also known as Youth Day across China.

3   During the Anti-Japanese War, Peking University moved to Kunming and formed the National Southwestern United University, along with Tsinghua University and Nankai University. In 1946, after World War II, Peking University moved back to Beijing. At that time, the university comprised six schools (Arts, Science, Law, Medicine, Engineering, and Agriculture), and a research institute for **humanities** (*n.* 人文学科). The total student enrollment grew up to 3,000.

4   Peking University is a comprehensive and national key university. The university consists of 30 colleges and 12 departments, with 100 **specialties** (*n.* 专业) for undergraduates, 221 specialties for Master's degree candidates and 199 specialties

for **Doctoral** (*adj.* 博士的) candidates. While still laying stress on basic sciences, the university has paid special attention to the development of applied sciences.

5   At present, Peking University has 216 research institutions and research centres, including 2 national engineering research centres, 81 key national disciplines, 12 national key **laboratories** (*n.* 实验室). With eight million holdings (*n.* 所有物), the university library is the largest of its kind in Asia.

6   Peking University has one of the largest pools of international students in China. Every year, Peking University has about 2,000 international students on campus. About 40% of the international students are Korean and the remaining 60% are made up of students from most countries in the world including most of Western Europe, North America, South America, all parts of Asia, Australia as well as many parts of Africa. The university is a member of Universitas 21, an international association of research-led universities.

7   The university has made an effort to combine the research on fundamental scientific issues with the training of personnel with high level specialized knowledge and professional skill as demanded by the country's modernization. It strives not only for the **simultaneous** (*adj.* 同时的) improvements in teaching and research work, but also for the promotion of **interaction** (*n.* 相互作用) and mutual promotion among various subjects.

8   Peking University is becoming a center for teaching and research, consisting of diverse branches of learning such as pure and applied sciences, social sciences and the humanities, and sciences of management and education. Its aim is to rank among the world's best universities in the near future.

(584 words)

Reading Comprehension

I. Answer the following questions according to the passage.

1. Why does Peking University celebrate her anniversary on May 4th?
2. What kind of university is Peking University?
3. What is the emphasis of the university?
4. More than one-third of the international students in Peking University are from the USA, aren't they?
5. What are the two main tasks of the university?

II. Translate into Chinese the following sentences taken from the passage.

1. In 1912, following the Xinhai Revolution, the Imperial Capital University was renamed the National Peking University.
2. The anti-imperialist and anti-feudal May 4th Movement in 1919 is the most important moment in the history of Peking University.
3. While still laying stress on basic sciences, the university has paid special attention to the development of applied sciences.
4. With eight million holdings, the university library is the largest of its kind in Asia.
5. Its aim is to rank among the world's best universities in the next couple of decades.

III. Fill in the blanks with the words or phrases listed in Words and Expressions to Learn. Change the form where necessary.

1. The _____ of that project has been finished.
2. He can't bear the _____ and strains of modern life.
3. The classroom was beautifully decorated by the students for the _____.
4. Here she is the very _____ we were talking about!

5. These fish _____ in weight from 3 pounds to 5 pounds.
6. We must ensure the _____ of drinking water.
7. All neighbor states must revise their policy _____.
8. The British Parliament _____ the House of Commons and the House of Lords.

Part IV Practical English

Certificates(证明)

证明书种类很多,有工作经历证明、工作经验证明、病情证明、留学生经济担保书、学业成绩证明书以及公证书等等,是用来证明一个人的身份、学历、婚姻状况、身体情况等或某一件事情的真实情况。证明信的写法通常也采用一般信件格式,但多省掉收信人的姓名、地址和结束用语。称呼多用 To Whom It May Concern 意即"有关负责人",但此项也可省略。写证明书要求言简意赅。

各种常见证明一般都有固定的开头,那就是 This is to certify that...

Sample I

Notarial Deed

(07) Shu Zi, No. 1130

May 2, 2006

This is to certify that Mr. Zhang Qianghong holds a diploma issued to him in 2004 by Chuanhua University (Diploma No. 04064) and that the seal of the said University and the signature by President Zhou Yansheng are authentic.

Chengdu Notary Public Office

Sichuan Province, the People's Republic of China

Notary: Li Dong

公证书

（07 蜀公证字第 1130 号）

兹证明张强洪先生持有川华大学于 2004 年发给他的 04064 号毕业文凭。文凭上的学校印章和校长周炎生的签字属实。

中华人民共和国
四川省成都市公证处
公证员：李东
2006 年 5 月 2 日

Sample II

Certificate

Zhang Hua, a student from Zhongnan University, having passed the yearly test of 2006 for non-computer majors in the knowledge and aptitude of computer application, is hereby conferred this certificate.

Test grade and language: Grade I, Windows

Sichuan Education Committee

Date: December 2006   Certificate No. 20063101090

证　明

中南大学学生张华参加 2006 年度普通高校非计算机专业学生计算机应用知识和应用能力等级考试，成绩合格，特授予此证书。

考试级别、语种：一级　Windows

四川省教育委员会
2006 年 12 月

证书编号：20063101090

Writing Practice

I. Complete the following certificate according to the Chinese version.

> **医生证明书**
>
> 兹证明病人托马斯先生,男,41岁,因患急性阑尾炎,于2006年6月9日住院。经立即施行手术和十天治疗后,现已痊愈,将于2006年6月19日出院。建议在家休息一个星期后再上班工作。
>
> 主治医生:杰克·霍普金斯
> (签名)
> 2006年6月18日

> **Doctor's Certificate**
>
> June 18, 2006
>
> This is to _____ (1) that our patient, Mr. Thomas, male, aged 41, was admitted into our hospital on June 9, 2006, for acute appendicitis. After immediate _____ (2) and ten days of _____ (3), he has completely _____ (4) and will be discharged on June 19, 2006. It is suggested that he _____ (5) for one week at home before _____ (6) back to his work.
>
> (Signature)
> Jack Hopkins
> Surgeon-in-charge

II. Translate into English the following certificate.

> **健康证明**
>
> 兹证明中环教育学院王洪江教授,男,62岁,身体健康,可以前往法国参加第九届国际数学统计学会议,特此证明。
>
> 广东省医院
> 主任医生:张 国
> (签名)
> 2006年9月21日

Part V English Salon

Jingles and Rhymes

(1) I passed by his garden, and marked with one eye
How the Owl and the Panther were sharing a pie:
The Panther took pie-crust and gravy, and meat,
While the Owl had the dish as its share of the treat.
When the pie was all finished, the Owl, as a boon,
Was kindly permitted to pocket the spoon,
While the Panther received knife and fork with a growl,
And concluded the banquet...

(2) Bill had a billboard, and Bill also had a board bill.
The board bill bored Bill, so that Bill sold the billboard to pay his board bill.
So after Bill sold his billboard to pay his board bill, the board bill no longer bored Bill.

Requirement

Read aloud and recite the above jingles and try to find the rhymes.

Unit Two

Part I TEXT

Guide to Text-Learning

1. Words and Expressions Related to the Topic

contemporary	同时代的人
desperate	绝望的；不顾一切的
exceptional	例外的；异常的
exclusive	排外的，独占的
fascination	魔力；入迷，强烈爱好
financially	财政上，金融上
hook	钩住；沉迷，上瘾
mathematical	数学的；精确的
obsession	迷住，困扰
overtake	赶上，追上
rigorous	严格的，严厉的；精确的
teletype	电传打字机；电报交换机
Noughts and Crosses	划井字游戏，圈叉游戏(在井字形九格中画○或×,先将三个连成一线者胜)

2. Grammatical Structures to Learn

(1) Funds were raised, mainly by parents, **which** enabled the school to gain access to a computer...

学校设立了基金，它主要来源于家长们，这使得计算机课程得以在学校开展。

(2) Bill Gates was immediately hooked—**so was his best friend at the time**, Kent Evans, and another student, Paul Allen, who was two years older than Bill.

比尔·盖茨立即被迷住了，当时他最好的朋友肯特·伊文斯以及比盖茨大两岁的保罗·艾伦也深深地被吸引了。

> **Warming-Up Questions:**
>
> 1. Do you know something about Bill Gates?
> 2. Was Bill Gates a common boy with average intelligence when he was nine or ten years old?
> 3. How was Bill Gates hooked by computing?

The Road to Success

1   As a child—and as an adult as well—Bill Gates was untidy. It has been said that in order to stop this, his mother Mary drew up plans for him in **detail**. Everything is arranged in time, at work or during his **leisure** time.

2   Bill's contemporaries, even at the age, recognized that he was exceptional. One of his friends recalled, "He was never a **nerd** or a **goof** or the kind of kid you didn't want in your team. We all knew Bill was smarter than us. Even back then, when he was nine or ten years old, he talked like an adult and could express himself in ways that none of us understood."

3   Bill was also well ahead of his classmates in mathematics and science. He needed to go to a school that **challenged** him. Then his parents sent him to Lakeside—an all-boys' school for exceptional students. It was Seattle's most exclusive school and was noted for its rigorous academic demands, a place where "even the **dumb** kids were smart."

4   Lakeside allowed students to **pursue** their own interests, to whatever **extent** they

---

detail /ˈdiːteil/ *n.*
an individual part or item
细目，细节

leisure /ˈliːʒə/ *n.*
freedom from time-consuming duties, responsibilities, or activities
空闲，闲暇

nerd /nəːd/ *n.*
a person regarded as stupid, inept, or unattractive
蠢货

goof /ɡuːf/ *n.*
an incompetent, foolish, or stupid person
傻瓜，笨蛋

challenge /ˈtʃælindʒ/ *n.&v.*
(a) call to engage in a contest, fight, or competition
挑战

dumb /dʌm/ *adj.*
incapable of using speech
哑的

pursue /pəˈsjuː/ *v.*
follow in an effort to overtake or capture; chase
为了赶上或捕获而努力跟随；追求

extent /iksˈtent/ *n.*
how large, important, or serious something is, etc.
范围；程度

wished. The school prided itself on making conditions and facilities **available** that would **enable** all its students to reach their full **potential**. It was the **ideal** environment for someone like Bill Gates. In 1968, the school made a decision that would change thirteen-year-old Bill Gates' life and that of many others, too.

5 Funds were raised, mainly by parents, which enabled the school to gain access to a computer—a Program Data Processor (PDP) —through a teletype machine. Type in a few instructions on the teletype machine and a few seconds later the PDP would type back its **response**. Bill Gates was immediately hooked—so was his best friend at the time, Kent Evans, and another student, Paul Allen, who was two years older than Bill.

6 Whenever they had free time, and sometimes when they didn't, they would dash over to the computer room to use the machine. The students became so single-minded that they soon overtook their teachers in knowledge about computing and got into a lot of trouble because of their obsession. They were **neglecting** their other studies—every piece of word was handed in late. Classes were cut. Computer time was also proving to be very expensive. Within months, the whole **budget** that had been set aside for the year had been used up.

7 At fourteen, Bill was already writing short programs for the computer to perform. Early game programs such as Tic-Tac-Toe, or Noughts and Crosses, and Lunar Landing were written in what was to become Bill's second language, BASIC.

8 If Bill Gates was going to be good at something, it was essential to be the best. Bill's and Paul's fascination with computers and the business world meant that they read a great deal. Paul enjoyed magazines like *Popular Electronics*. Computer

---

available /əˈveɪləbl/ *adj.*
present and ready for use; accessible; obtainable
可用的；可获得的，可得到的

enable /ɪˈneɪbl/ *v.*
make it possible for someone to do something, or for something to happen
使能够

potential /pəˈtenʃ(ə)l/ *adj.*
capable of being but not yet in existence
潜在的，可能的
n.
inherent ability or capacity for growth, development, or coming into being
潜力

ideal /aɪˈdɪəl/ *adj.*
the best or most suitable that something could possibly be
理想的

response /rɪsˈpɒns/ *n.*
a reaction, as that of an organism or a mechanism, to a specific stimulus
反应

neglect /nɪˈɡlekt/ *v.*
pay too little attention to something
忽视，疏忽

budget /ˈbʌdʒɪt/ *n.*
a sum of money allocated for a particular purpose
预算

time was expensive and, because both boys were desperate to get more time and because Bill already had an insight into what they could achieve financially, the two of them decided to set themselves up as a company: The Lakeside Programmers Group. "Let's call the real world and try to sell something to it!" Bill announced.

(590 words)

Phrases and Useful expressions

in detail	all the separate features and pieces of information about sth	详细地
to... extent	used to say how true sth is or how great an effect or change is	在……角度、范围、方面
dash over	go or run somewhere very quickly	冲向
set sth aside	keep sth, especially money, time, or a particular area, for a special purpose	留出
set sth up	start a company, organization, committee	建立
use up	use all of sth	用完,耗尽
have an insight into	a sudden clear understanding of sth or part of sth, especially a complicated situation or idea	了解,熟悉,看透,识破
pride yourself on (doing) sth	be especially proud of sth that you do well, or of a good quality that you have	引以为豪
be desperate to do sth	need or want sth very much	为……不顾一切
draw up	prepare for sth	准备好,提前打算

Notes

1. Bill's contemporaries, even at the age, recognized that he was exceptional. 比尔的同代，即使在当时那么小的年纪，都能看出他是与众不同的。

   even at the age 在这里为插入语，是对前句的补充，加强语气。

2. Funds were raised, mainly by parents, which enabled the school to gain access to a computer... 学校设立了基金，它主要来源于家长们，这使得计算机课程得以在学校开展。

   mainly by parents 在这里为插入语，是对前句的解释说明。

   which 在本句引导的是非限制性定语从句，先行词为 funds。

3. Bill Gates was immediately hooked—so was his best friend at the time, Kent Evans, and another student, Paul Allen, who was two years older than Bill. 比尔·盖茨立即被迷住了，当时他最好的朋友肯特·伊文斯以及比比尔大两岁的保罗·艾伦也深深地被吸引了。

   so was his best fried at the time 在本句是 so 引导的倒装，表示与前面的情况相同。

   同样的例子还有：

   I finished my homework, so did he.
   Jane works hard, so does her sister.

# Exercises

Reading Aloud and Memorizing the Following

I. Read aloud the following paragraph taken from the text until you learn it by heart.

   Whenever they had free time, and sometimes when they didn't, they would dash over to the computer room to use the machine. The students became so single-minded that they soon overtook their teachers in knowledge about computing and got into a lot of trouble because of their obsession. They were neglecting their other studies—every piece of word was handed in late. Classes were cut. Computer time was also proving to be very expensive. Within months, the whole budget that had been set aside for the year had been used up.

Comprehension of the Text

II. Choose the best answer to each of the following questions according to the passage.

1. What is the main idea of the text?
   A. How Bill Gates became rich.
   B. How Bill Gates set up his Microsoft Company.
   C. How Bill Gates learned computer.
   D. How Bill Gates and his friends led his way to success.

2. How did Bill's contemporaries think of him?
   A. They thought Bill was a nerd.
   B. They thought Bill was a goof.
   C. They thought Bill was outstanding.
   D. They thought Bill was a dumb boy.

3. What kind of school was Lakeside like in Seattle?
   A. Lakeside was the school which allowed students to pursue their interests.

B. Lakeside was an all-boy school.

C. Lakeside was the school which prides itself on making conditions and facilities available that would enable all its students to reach their full potential.

D. All above.

4. What does "Computer time was expensive, both boys were desperate to get more time" mean in the last paragraph?

   A. Bill and Paul felt hopeless because they didn't have time to play computer game.

   B. Bill and Paul felt hopeless because they didn't have money to buy a computer.

   C. Bill and Paul were willing to do anything to get more time.

   D. Bill and Paul were willing to do anything to get a computer.

5. What can we learn from the text?

   A. We young people should learn computer well.

   B. We young people should follow our interests.

   C. We young people should try every means to achieve our goal.

   D. We young people should learn something by heart.

III. Answer the following questions with the information you've got from the text.

1. Why did Bill's mother draw up plans for him in detail?   (Para.1)
2. How was Bill's performance in mathematics and science?   (Para. 3)
3. Where did Lakeside get funds to gain access to a computer?   (Para. 5)
4. What was Bill able to do with computer when he was 14 years old?   (Para. 7)
5. How did Bill and Paul achieve their financial goal with computers?   (Para. 8)

Vocabulary

IV. Spell out the words with the help of the given definitions and the first letters.

1. a place where people stay in tents, shelters, etc., for a short time, usually in the mountains, a forest, etc. (c_____)

2. be especially proud of something that you do well, or of a good quality that you have (p_____)

3. a curved piece of metal or plastic that you use for hanging things on (h _____)
4. relating to the moon or to travel to the moon (l _____)
5. careful, thorough, and exact (r _____)
6. obtain or achieve sth you want or need (g _____)
7. information in a form that can be stored and used, especially on a computer (d _____)
8. power of learning, understanding and reasoning (i _____)
9. relating to money or the management of money (f _____)
10. clothes considered as a group (c _____)

V. Fill in the blanks with the words given below. Change the form where necessary.

| able | pursuit | rigour | hook | potential |
| fascination | perform | exception | education | exclusion |

1. Different children have different _____ needs.
2. Promotion in the first year is only given in _____ circumstances.
3. Every new drug has to pass a series of _____ safety checks before it is put on sale.
4. He was _____ to discover that they had both been born in the same town on the same day.
5. People have to move to other areas in _____ of work.
6. Our figure skating club has _____ use of the rink on Mondays.
7. Have you ever heard a live _____ of Beethoven's Seventh Symphony?
8. He completed the job to the best of his _____ .
9. I _____ a 20-pound salmon last week.
10. For the first time she realized the _____ danger of her situation.

VI. Fill in the blanks with proper prepositions or adverbs.
1. As a nation we pride ourselves _____ our strong sense of sportsmanship and fair play.
2. She was desperate _____ fear.
3. Draw _____ a list of all the things you want to do.

33

4. This issue will be discussed _____ detail in Chapter 5.
5. We all _____ some extent remember the good times and forget the bad.
6. Try to set _____ some time each day for exercise.
7. She's used _____ all the hot water.
8. The article gives us a real insight _____ the causes of the present economic crisis.
9. They want to set _____ their own import-export business.
10. Olive dashed _____ the room, grabbed her bag, and ran out again.

Structure

VII. Rewrite the following sentences after the models.

Model 1 Bill Gates was immediately hooked—**so was his best friend at the time**, Kent Evans, and another student, Paul Allen, who was two years older than Bill.

1. I went to Japan last year. Kate went to Japan, too.
2. He likes football. His father likes football, too.
3. Jack was interested in math. His sister was interested in math, too.
4. Tom climbed the hill yesterday. Jim climbed the hill yesterday, too.
5. He is very diligent. They are diligent, too.

Model 2 Funds were raised, mainly by parents, **which** enabled the school to gain access to a computer.

1. Yesterday he brought two books. These were written by a young Chinese writer. (which)
2. She took care of the little boy. His parents had gone abroad. (whose)
3. Three days later he arrived at the village. He was to stay for a month there. (where)
4. The house belonged to Mr. Wilson. It was burnt down. (which)
5. The girls are from that college. They are dancing in the hall. (who)

VIII. Translate the following sentences into Chinese.

1. One of his friends recalled, "He was never a nerd or a goof or the kind of kid you didn't want in your team."

2. It was Seattle's most exclusive school and was noted for its rigorous academic demands, a place where "even the dumb kids were smart."

3. The school prided itself on making conditions and facilities available that would enable all its students to reach their full potential. It was the ideal environment for someone like Bill Gates.

4. The students became so single-minded that they soon overtook their teachers in knowledge about computing and got into a lot of trouble because of their obsession.

5. If Bill Gates was going to be good at something, it was essential to be the best.

IX. Translate the following sentences into English using the words or phrases in the brackets.

1. 我在一定程度上同意他的计划。(to some extent)

2. 你能详细为我们描述你在美国的生活吗？(in detail)

3. 每次去超市前我都要列一个购物清单。(draw up)

4. 他对可能发生的事情了如指掌。(have an insight into)

5. 她为自己能讲多种外国语而感到自豪。(pride oneself on)

Part II Grammar

Tenses(时态)(三)

时态(三)完成时(Perfect Tenses)

1. 现在完成时(Present Perfect Tense)

1) 构成:have/has+ 过去分词。现在完成时的肯定式、否定式和疑问式列表如下(以 work 为例):

	肯定句	否定句	疑问句
单数	I have worked You have worked She/He/It has worked	I have not worked You have not worked She/He/It has not worked	Have I worked Have you worked Has she/he/it worked
复数	We have worked You have worked They have worked	We have not worked You have not worked They have not worked	Have we worked Have you worked Have they worked

2) 用法:

a. 表示过去发生的某一动作对现在造成的影响或产生的结果。强调过去的动作与现在的联系,即强调对现在的影响和结果。例如:

　　Someone has broken the window. 有人把窗子打破了。("打破"这一动作在说话以前就已经完成,而结果或影响至今仍然存在,其结果是 the window is now broken。)

　　I have lost my pen. 我把钢笔丢了。(结果是:I have no pen to use.)

　　He has locked the door. 他把门锁上了。(结果是:Now the door is locked and we can't go in.)

　　The party has started. 晚会已经开始了。(The party started and it is now going on.)

　　She has not eaten anything today. 她今天什么都没吃。(She must be hungry now.)

b. 表示一个开始于过去,持续到现在,并可能继续下去的动作或状态,常和 for, since 引导的时间状语连用。(for 是介词,后面只能跟单词或词组;since 是介词或连词,后面可以跟单词、词组或句子)。可用于 how long... 的句型中,表示持续的时间。例如:

He has studied English for ten years. 他学习英语已经十年了。(可能继续学下去)

She has lived here since 1990. 她自 1990 年就住在这里了。(也许还在这儿住)

He has been in Nanjing since 1989. 他自 1989 年就在南京了。(现在可能还在)

How long have you lived in the house? 你在这所房子里住了多久了?(从过去到现在)

2. 过去完成时 (Past Perfect Tense)

1) 构成:had+ 过去分词(had 用于所有人称)。过去完成时的肯定式、否定式和疑问式列表如下(以 work 为例):

		肯定句	否定句	疑问句
单数		I had worked You had worked She/He/It had worked	I had not worked You had not worked She/He/It had not worked	Had I worked Had you worked Had she/he/it worked
复数		We had worked You had worked They had worked	We had not worked You had not worked They had not worked	Had we worked Had you worked Had they worked

2) 用法

a. 表示在过去某一段时间或某一动作之前完成的动作或已经存在的状态,也就是过去的过去。过去完成时的过去时间可用以下四种方式表达:

(1) 用 by 或 before 引导的短语表示,如 by that time, by... o'clock, by the end of..., before 1993 等。

By three o'clock yesterday afternoon we had finished the work.
到昨天下午三点钟,我们已经做完了工作。

(2) 用 when 和 before 引导的时间状语从句表示:

I had seen her before she saw me.
在她看见我之前,我已经看到她了。

(3) 用 he said, he knew, he asked 等宾语从句表示:

He said he had never been to Paris.
他说他从来没到过巴黎。

(4) 通过上下文表示：

I was very sad at his death. We had been good friends since our childhood.
他的去世让我很难过。我们打小就是好朋友。

b. 表示过去某一时间之前发生的动作或存在的状态一直持续到过去的某一时间，并可能继续下去，常和 for 或 since 引导的表示一段时间的短语或从句连用。例如：

By the end of last month he had worked in Shanghai for twenty years.
到上月底，他已经在上海工作了整整 20 年。（可能继续工作下去）

3. 将来完成时 (Future Perfect Tense)

1) 构成：shall/will+ have+ 过去分词（shall 用于第一人称，美国英语中 will 用于所有人称）

2) 用法：表示将来某个时间之前已经完成了的动作，句中必有一个表示将来的特定时间。例如：

You will have reached Shanghai by this time tomorrow.
明天这个时候你就到上海了。

By ten o'clock this evening I shall have reviewed my lessons.
到今晚十点，我就将复习完功课了。

3) 注意：在时间或条件状语从句中，如果要表示将来完成的动作，要用现在完成时来代替将来完成时。试比较：

I shall take a rest when I shall have finished the job.（错误）

I shall take a rest when I have finished the job.（正确）

If you will have got the letter this time tomorrow, please let me know.（错误）

If you have got the letter this time tomorrow, please let me know.（正确）

4. 过去将来完成时 (Past Future Perfect Tense)

1) 构成："should/would+ have + 动词过去分词"

2) 用法：过去将来完成时主要表示从过去某时看将来某时就已完成的动作。如：

I thought she would have told you about it.
我想她可能已经告诉你了。

Exercises

I. Complete each of the following sentences with the most appropriate word or words from the four choices marked A, B, C and D.

1. Poor Frank! He _____ ill since last Friday.
   A. has felt   B. have felt   C. feel   D. felt

2. Tom _____ back from France. Yesterday he _____ about it.
   A. just comes; told   B. has just come; told me
   C. came just; was told me   D. just has come; was telling

3. In the past five years, Robert _____ England twice.
   A. visit   B. visits   C. visiting   D. has visited

4. Maria hasn't visited her home in Spain _____.
   A. for many years   B. since many years
   C. many years since   D. many years ago

5. By next Saturday Tom _____ a whole month without smoking a cigarette.
   A. will go   B. will have gone
   C. has gone   D. has been going

6. If the horse wins today, he _____ thirty races in the last five years.
   A. will win   B. will have won
   C. would have won   D. had won

7. We _____ supper when a policeman came to the door.
   A. just have had   B. had had just
   C. have just had   D. had just had

8. By the time he reached the dentist, the pain in his tooth _____.
   A. stopped   B. had stopped
   C. has stopped   D. has been stopped

9. The old man _____ for three days when his son got back home.
   A. has been dead   B. had been dead
   C. died   D. had died

10. He said that he _____ another try.
    A. will have   B. will do   C. would have   D. would do

39

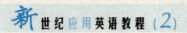

II. **Fill in the blanks with the proper tense.**

1. Don't look for the basketball, Henry _____ (take) it away.
2. The teacher _____ (devote) all his life to teaching.
3. I _____ (mean) to help him with his English last Saturday, but I was too busy then.
4. I _____ (invite) her to the party before I went to Paris for business.
5. I wonder who _____ (break) my window? It can't be John.
6. Mr. Brown _____ (work) in Beijing since 1993.
7. Mother isn't in; she _____ (go) to the store.
8. The teacher asked the students if they _____ (finish) their homework.
9. She returned to the shop to buy the skirt, but found that they _____ (sell) it.
10. When I saw her smiling, I knew she _____ (have) good news of her son.
11. We _____ (finish) the task at this time tomorrow.
12. He said that he _____ (arrive) home six hours later.

Part III Reading Practice

Guide to Reading

1. Words and Expressions to Learn

score	n.&v.	the number of points that each team or player has won in a game or competition	得分
competitive	adj.	trying very hard to be more successful than other people	有竞争意识的
dominate	v.	control or have more importance than other people or things	支配；占优势
occasion	n.	a time when something happens	场合；时机，机会
rival	n.	a person, group, or organization that you compete with in sport, a fight, etc.	竞争者，对手
infinitely	adv.	very much used especially when comparing things	无限地，无穷地
physical	adj.	related to someone's body rather than their minds or emotions	身体的
come into sth		be involved in something	进入状态

2. Pre-Reading Questions

(1) How well do you know about Michael Jordan?

(2) What reason do you think makes Jordan so unique and brilliant?

The God in Youth

1   There were already **signs** (征兆,迹象)that he had a good deal of talent. Harvest Smith, a classmate and close friend who in those days played basketball with him **practically**(事实上,实际上) every day, thought he was the best player on their ninth-grade team—he was small, but he was very quick. "You'd see him **get a shot off** (投篮,射篮), and you'd wonder how he did it, because he wasn't that big," Smith said, "but it was the quickness. The only question was how big he was going to be—and how far up he would take his skill level."

2   The summer after ninth grade, Jordan and Smith both went to **Pop** (*adj.* 普遍的,流行的) Herring's basketball camp. Neither of them had yet come into his body, and almost all of the **varsity** (*n.* 大学运动代表队) players, two and sometimes three years older, seemed infinitely stronger at that moment when a year or two in physical development can make all the difference. In Smith's mind there was no doubt which of the two of them was the better player—it was Michael **by far** (到目前为止). But on the day the varsity cuts were announced—it was the big day of the year, for they had all known for weeks when the list would be posted—he and Roy Smith had gone to the Laney **gym** (*n.* 体育馆). Smith's name was on it, Michael's was not.

3   It was the worst day of Jordan's young life. The list was **alphabetical** (*adj.* 按字母顺序的), so he focused on where the Js should be, and it wasn't there, and he kept reading and rereading the list, hoping somehow that he had missed it, or that the alphabetical listing had been done incorrectly. That day he went home by himself and went to his room and cried. Smith understood what was happening—Michael, he knew, never wanted you to see him when he was hurt. "We knew Michael was good," Fred Lynch, the Laney assistant coach, said later, "but we wanted him to play more and we thought the **jayvee** (*n.* 大学运动队第二队(队员)) was better for him." He easily became the best player on the jayvee that year. He

simply dominated the play, and he did it not by size but with quickness. There were games in which he would score forty points. He was so good, in fact, that the jayvee games became quite popular. The entire varsity began to come early so they could watch him play in the jayvee games.

4   Smith noticed that while Jordan had been wildly competitive before he had been cut, after the cut he seemed even more competitive than ever, as if determined that it would never happen again. His **coaches** (*n.* 教练) noticed it, too. "The first time I ever saw him, I had no idea who Michael Jordan was. I was helping to coach the Laney varsity," said Ron Coley. "We went over to Goldsboro, which was our big rival, and I entered the gym when the jayvee game was just ending up. There were nine players on the **court** (*n.* 球场) just **coasting** (*v.* 无目的地或用很小力地运动), but there was one kid playing his heart out. The way he was playing I thought his team was down one point with two minutes to play. So I looked up at the clock and his team was down twenty points and there was only one minute to play. It was Michael, and I quickly learned he was always like that."

5   Between the time he was cut and the start of basketball in his junior year, Jordan grew about four inches. The speed had always been there, and now he was stronger, and he could **dunk** (*v.* 灌篮). His hands had gotten much bigger, Smith noticed. He was as driven as ever, the hardest-working player on the team **in practice** (在实践中，实际上). If he thought that his teammates were not working hard enough, he would get on them himself, and **on occasion** (有时，偶然) he pushed the coaches to get on them. Suddenly Laney High had the beginning of a very good basketball team, and its rising star was Michael Jordan.

(660 words)

Exercises

Reading Comprehension

I. Read the following statements carefully, and decide whether they are true (T) or false (F) according to the passage.

1. Michael Jordan was one of the greatest basketball players, for he was very tall since early on. ( )
2. Pop Herring's basketball camp accepted Michael Jordan immediately. ( )
3. When he knew he was out of the list, Michael Jordan was hurt. ( )
4. Michael Jordan was soon a member of jayvee because he had a big size. ( )
5. Because of his competitiveness, Michael Jordan caught the eyes of his coach. ( )
6. Michael Jordan caught the eyes of his coach because he was the one who played by heart. ( )
7. Laney High became one of the best basketball team because Michael Jordan was the leader. ( )
8. Michael Jordan was the rising star owing to his quickness and devotion to basketball. ( )

II. Fill in the blanks with the words or phrases listed in Word and Expressions to Learn. Change the form where necessary.

1. Anyone who _____ under 70 percent will have to retake the exam.
2. New machinery has enhanced the company's productivity and _____.
3. It was obvious that her husband completely _____ her.
4. I didn't know Terry very well, but we went out for a(n) _____ drink together.
5. The two teams have always been _____.
6. It's difficult to really imagine a(n) _____ universe.
7. Josie doesn't _____ the movie until quite near the end.
8. A lot of British people avoid _____ contact with strangers.

Part IV Practical English

Credentials & Certifications(证书与证件)

1. 毕业证书

毕业证书一般都有校长签名，所以正文的开头都以校长的身份来证明某某学生准予从该校毕业，常用 I hereby certify that(兹证明……)。

Sample

GRADUATION CERTIFICATE

  I hereby certify that **Zhang Xiaojun**, male, born on **May 2,1984**, was a student of the English major in the Department of Foreign Language & Literature and, having completed the four years' courses from September 2002 through July 2006 and fulfilled all the requirements prescribed by the department, graduated from Sichuan Tianyuan University in July 2006.

N0. 0601364

PHOTO

Sichuan Tianyuan University
  (Signature)
  President
Issued on July 10, 2006

毕业证书

第 0601364 号

学生 张小军,性别 男,一九八四年五月二日生,二零零二年九月至二零零六年七月 在本校 外语系英语专业 学习,修业期满,成绩合格,准予毕业。

照片

四川天元大学
校长
(签名)
二零零六年七月十日

2. 学生证

Sample

NO. 0201364

PHOTO

Sichuan Tianyuan University
Issued on September, 2002

Certificate

Zhang Xiaojun, male, born in May, 1984, having passed National College Entrance Examination, was enrolled in **Department of Foreign Language & Literature**, Sichuan Tianyuan University in September, 2002, majoring in English. The length of schooling is four years.

Sichuan Tianyuan University
Date of Certification: September, 2002

```
                    学生证
第 0201364 号      张小军，男，一九八四年五月
                    出生。于二零零二 年 九 月经全国
    照片            普通高等学校入学考试录取进入
                    我校 外语系英语 专业学习，学制
                    四 年。
四川天元大学
二零零二 年 九 月                        四川天元大学
                                         二零零二 年 九 月
```

此类证件正文的开头常用以下套语：

1. This is to certify that...	兹证明……
2. I have the pleasure in certifying that...	我乐于证明……
3. It is my pleasure to certify that...	我乐于证明……
4. I hereby certify that...	我证明……
5. Let it be known that...	兹证明……

Complete the following certificate according to the Chinese version.

```
              毕业证书
                        第 8301364 号
   学生马宏博，男，一九六三年六月出生，一九七九年九月进
入本校外国语言文学系英语专业，学习四年，完成全部学业，成
绩合格，准予毕业，此证。
                              校长
                             （签名）
                              朱久泗
                           四川天元大学
                           一九八三年七月
```

CERTIFICATE OF GRADUATION

Certificate No. 8301364

This is to _____ (1) that Ma Hongbo, male, born in June 1963, was _____ (2) in Department of Foreign Language & Literature in September 1979, _____ (3) in English Language, having passed all the _____ (4) examinations and thesis, _____ (5) in July 1983.

(Signature)

Zhu Jiusi

President

Sichuan Tianyuan University

Date of issue: July 1983

Part V   English Salon

Riddles

1. If you drop a white hat into the Red Sea, what does it become?
2. What starts with E, ends with E and only has one letter?
3. Who earns a living by driving his customers away?
4. What two things can't you have for breakfast?
5. What goes on four legs at dawn, two at noon, and three at dusk?

Unit Three

Part I TEXT

 Guide to Text-Learning

1. Words and Expressions Related to the Topic

graduate	大学毕业生
enterprise	事业单位,公司
apply	申请
position	位置,职位
job market	就业市场
job fair	就业见面会
job hunting	找工作
job interview	求职面试
employment	就业;职业
employment agency	职业介绍所
enrollment expansion	扩招
institutions of higher learning	高校

2. Grammatical Structures to Learn

(1) College graduates **tend to** concentrate their job searches in economically developed cities ...

大学毕业生大都倾向于在经济发达地区找工作……

(2) Local governments and universities nationwide are active in **doing their part to** create a favorable environment for the employment of graduates.

全国各地方政府和大学都在各尽其职,积极努力为大学毕业生就业创造一个良好的环境。

(3) Apart from the pay factor, they **base their choices on** the fact that large

enterprises can provide them with more stable benefits and employment security.

除了工资方面的因素，大公司企业能给他们提供更加稳定的福利待遇和工作安全感，这便是他们择业的依据和基础。

Warming-Up Questions:

1. Are you as anxious about the employment situation as today's college graduates?
2. What are your concepts of employment?

Employment Challenge to College Students

1   Today's university graduates usually have great pressure in finding fairly good jobs. They feel a **chill** in the employment market.

2   The recent years have **witnessed** the great **leap** in the number of college graduates since Chinese institutions of higher learning began expanding enrollment in 1999, which has made the employment situation very **severe**. College enrollment has expanded at a faster rate than the job market, limiting graduates' employment opportunities. The newly emerging urban labor force, the **surplus** rural laborers entering urban areas for work, and **laid-off** workers waiting for reemployment combine to pressure the employment market, making the situation more severe.

3   However, the expansion in college enrollment is not the only cause of the tight job market. There are multiple factors. Some universities and colleges have been

---

chill /tʃil/ n.
coldness; feeling of gloom and depression
寒冷；(心情)冰冷，阴沉

witness /'witnis/ v.
be present at sth and see it
目击，见证

leap /li:p/ n.
jump; rapid change or increase
跳；激增；骤变

severe /si'viə/ adj.
very bad, intense, difficult
非常恶劣、紧张、困难

surplus /'sə:pləs/ adj.
more than is needed or used
剩余的，过剩的

laid-off /leid-ɔf/ adj.
dismissed from the work
下岗

lured to expand enrollment of some popular **specialties** such as accounting and law without consideration of changes in market demand. This has **saturated** market demand, leaving the **beneficiaries** of the enrollment expansion in these specialties to **confront** job-hunting difficulties and a sense of loss.

4   Employers are now **shifting** their focus from academic background to practical abilities of graduates. However, college education in China puts more emphasis on academics than on skills. This results in a strange phenomenon: Employers have difficulties **recruiting** qualified graduates, while many graduates remain unemployed.

5   In addition, many graduates do not know how to prepare job interviews. An analysis of graduates' **resumes** has found that more than 80 percent of the resumes are **deficient**, often missing points that are essential for a resume. This indicates that graduating students generally lack career **awareness** and employment **know-how**, which creates **obstacles** in their job-hunting.

6   The concentration of job locations is another factor causing difficulties. College graduates tend to concentrate their job searches on economically developed cities, such as Beijing, Shanghai, Guangzhou and Shenzhen, and southeastern coastal areas, and favor government institutions, foreign-funded companies and large enterprises. Few of them are interested in economically underdeveloped regions, small towns or rural areas, and

---

lure /ljuə/ v.
attract or attempt sb
吸引，诱惑

specialty /'speʃlti/ n.
interest, activity, subject, etc. in which a person majors
专业；特长

saturate /'sætʃəreit/ v.
make sth wet; fill sb/sth completely with sth
浸湿；充满某物

beneficiary /ˌbeni'fiʃəri/ n.
a person who receives sth or who benefits from sth
受益者，受惠者

confront /kən'frʌnt/ v.
face
面对，面临

shift /ʃift/ v.
change from one position or direction to another
改变位置或方向

recruit /ri'kru:t/ v.
gain sb as new member
吸收某人为新成员，招募

resume /'rezju:mei/ n.
brief account of sb's previous career, usu. submitted with an application for a job
个人简历，履历

deficient /di'fiʃənt/ adj.
incomplete, inadequate
不完全的；不完美的；不充足的

awareness /ə'weənis/ n.
having realization of sth, be conscious of sth
意识

know-how /nəu-hau/ n.
practical knowledge or skill in an activity
实践知识或技术；本事；技能

obstacle /'ɔbstəkl/ n.
thing in the way that either stops or makes it difficult
障碍，妨碍物

many have a **discriminative** attitude towards small and medium-sized enterprises. Apart from the pay factor, they base their choices on the fact that large enterprises can provide them with more stable benefits and employment security.

7   The severe employment situation facing college graduates has drawn the attention of the government. Special measures have been **formulated** to expand the employment channels for graduates. For instance, cities are called on to relax residence registration restrictions to let in college graduates. It is suggested that service institutions be set up to offer career guidance to graduating students, and that a graduation employment information system be established to offer relevant information in a timely manner. The measures also include policies to encourage and support college graduates to look for work in **grass-roots** units and the western regions. Local governments and universities nationwide are active in doing their part to create a **favorable** environment for the employment of graduates.

8   We can predict that there will be more favorable policy environment for employment. Moreover, the development of the Chinese economy will help create more job opportunities. Therefore, graduating students, though facing a severe situation, need not worry too much. However, they should adjust their **mentality** and employment concepts. Once they do this, it will not be too difficult for them to find a job.

(551 words)

---

discriminative /dɪsˈkrɪmɪnətɪv/ *adj.*
being biased against sth
不公平的, 歧视的

formulate /ˈfɔːmjuleɪt/ *v.*
create sth in a precise form, make
使形式固定, 制定

grass-roots /ˈgrɑːsˈruːts/ *n.*
ordinary people
平民, 群众, 基层

favorable /ˈfeɪvərəbl/ *adj.*
helpful, suitable, good
有帮助的, 合适的, 良好的

mentality /menˈtælɪti/ *n.*
characteristic attitude of mind; way of thinking
心态, 精神状态

Useful Expressions

result in	have a specialized effect or consequence	产生某种作用或结果

provide sb with sth	offer sth to sb	向某人提供某物,供给,供应
call on	appeal to or urge sb to do sth	恳求或促使某人做某事

Notes

1 The recent years have witnessed the great leap in the number of college graduates since Chinese institutions of higher learning began expanding enrollment in 1999. 自1999年中国高校开始扩招以来,大学毕业生的数量近年来急剧猛增。

此句中应注意"时间段作主语+witness"的用法。当表达在一段时间内,某事、某方面或领域经历了或发生了很大变化,取得了新的发展时,便可使用此句型,例如:

The past 20 years have witnessed the rapid development of China's economy.

The past years have witnessed the resurgence of grammar in the language classroom.

2 College enrollment has expanded at a faster rate than the job market, limiting graduates' employment opportunities. 大学扩招的速度比就业市场的扩大要快,这便限制了毕业生的就业机会。

limiting 在此是 -ing 分词作状语,表示结果。

3 However, college education in China puts more emphasis on academics than on skills. 然而,中国的大学教育对学术知识学习的重视程度远大于技能的培养。

本句中 put emphasis on 意思是"把重点放在……上;重视"。put 可替换成 lay, place。英语中表达相同意思的结构还有:attach importance to, lay/place focus on, set store by。

4 Employers have difficulties recruiting qualified graduates, while many graduates remain unemployed. 用人方很难招聘到合格的毕业生,而

很多毕业生又找不到工作。

本句中 have difficulty doing sth 是一常见句型，课文第一段中...have great pressure in finding... 也属同类句型。类似的结构还有:have trouble doing sth。

5. It is suggested that service institutions be set up to offer career guidance to graduating students ... 有人提议建立服务机构为毕业生提供职业指导……

It is suggested that sb. (should) do sth. 这是一个含虚拟语气的句子。表示命令或建议的动词 suggest, insist, propose, desire, demand, request, order, command 等常用于此句型中。例如：

It is ordered that the work should be done on time.

6. Once they do this, it will not be too difficult for them to find a job. 只要他们做到了这一点，找工作也就不再那么艰难了。

Once 在此用作连词，引导条件状语从句。

Reading Aloud and Memorizing the Following

I. Read the following paragraph taken from the text until you learn it by heart.

    The recent years have witnessed the great leap in the number of college graduates since Chinese institutions of higher learning began expanding enrollment in 1999, which has made the employment situation very severe. College enrollment has expanded at a faster rate than the job market, limiting graduates' employment opportunities. The newly emerging urban labor force, the surplus rural laborers entering urban areas for work, and laid-off workers waiting for reemployment combine to pressure the employment market, making the situation more severe.

Comprehension of the Text

II. Choose the best answer to each of the following questions according to the passage.

1. It is implied in the text that colleges should adjust and determine the enrollment in accordance with _____.
   A. the number of specialties
   B. students' choices
   C. students' academic background
   D. market demand

2. According to the text, which of the following is not the factor of employment problem?
   A. Personnel and residence registration system.
   B. Enrollment expansion of certain specialties.
   C. Graduates' lack in experience.
   D. Graduates' expectation on pay.

3. Employers have problem recruiting good graduates because _____.
   A. graduates haven't obtained good academic results
   B. graduates' resumes are inadequate
   C. graduates are not skillfully qualified
   D. graduates' majors don't fit in with jobs provided

4. The deficiency of graduates' resumes suggests that _____.
   A. graduates should be careful in writing their resumes
   B. graduates should try to improve their employment know-how
   C. graduates should prepare enough copies of their resumes
   D. graduates should restructure their resumes

5. With the implementation of measures and the development of China's economy, we can infer that _____.
   A. there will be more job opportunities for college graduates
   B. all college students can find jobs easily
   C. more college graduates are needed to meet market demand
   D. the employment problem will be satisfactorily solved

III. Answer the following questions with the information you've got from the text.

1. What change has taken place with regard to graduate employment situation? (Para. 1)
2. How does educational or institutional policy affect the employment situation? (Para. 2—3)
3. What are the common employment concepts of today's college graduates? Are they favorable or unfavorable? (Para. 6)
4. What measures have been taken to deal with the employment problem? (Para. 7)
5. What should college students do to adapt themselves to the changes in employment situation? (Para. 8)

Vocabulary

IV. Spell out the words with the help of the given definitions and the first letters.

1. most important (e _____)
2. make sth less severe; ease (a _____)
3. try (e _____)
4. incomplete (d _____)
5. force or weight of sth pressing on or against sth it touches (p _____)
6. focus attention intensively on sth, not thinking about other things (c _____)
7. good enough for a purpose (s _____)
8. usually theoretical, not practical (a _____)
9. interest or subject to which one gives particular attention or in which he majors (s _____)
10. a brief description of one's personal information, education and working experience, etc. (r _____)

V. Fill in the blanks with the words given below. Change the form when necessary.

confront	shift	deficient	witness	discriminative
know-how	recruit	formulate	awareness	favor

1. I don't think you are _____ how serious the problem is.
2. Don't _____ the responsibility onto others. You should do it yourself.

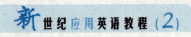

3. The past 20 years have _____ the rapid development of computer science.
4. Many children in rural areas are suffering from a _____ in vitamins.
5. That newly-established club is _____ new members.
6. The difficulties _____ us will certainly be overcome if we unite together and take actions against them.
7. Sexual _____ is one of the factors that cause difficulty for women to find employment.
8. Mrs. Brown always _____ Cathy.
9. A set of policies has been _____ to help those drop-outs to return to schools.
10. The mastery of negotiation _____ makes it possible for him to become a successful businessman.

VI. Fill in the blanks with proper prepositions or adverbs.

1. A group of doctor has been sent to the countryside to provide medical service _____ farmers.
2. I cannot concentrate _____ my studies with all that noise going on.
3. We had no difficulty _____ finding the hotel.
4. Society still discriminates _____ women.
5. Emphasis had been placed _____ the explanation and practice of grammatical rules in the traditional language classroom.
6. When faced _____ these problems, he felt nervous and didn't know what to do.
7. Is money essential _____ happiness?
8. The company had to lay _____ 25 employees because of production slowdown.
9. You may not be aware _____ your breathing and heart beating.
10. The factory produces cars _____ the rate of 10 per day.

Structure

VII. Rewrite the following sentences after the models.

Model 1 College graduates **are inclined to** concentrate their job searches on economically developed cities...

College graduates **tend to** concentrate their job searches on economically developed cities...

1. It has a tendency to rain a lot here in summer.
2. I'm inclined to go to bed early during the winter.
3. People are disposed to get fat as they grow older.
4. He's a good salesman, but his offhand manner is inclined to put people off.
5. Women are hopeful to live longer than men.

Model 2 Local governments and universities nationwide are active in **doing their share to** create a favorable environment for the employment of graduates.

Local governments and universities nationwide are active in **doing their part to** create a favorable environment for the employment of graduates.

1. If everyone will promise to do his duty, the program will certainly be a success.
2. I'll do my role to make it work.
3. I have done all I should do to persuade him and I can do no more.
4. We each perform our function to keep the house clean.
5. He has made an important contribution to solving this problem.

VIII. Study the model and translate the following sentences into English, by using the phrase "base ... on ..."

Model Apart from the pay factor, they **base their choices on** the fact that large enterprises can provide them with more stable benefits and employment security.

1. 她根据报告做出了她的结论。
2. 他刚完成了一部以畅销小说为题材的影片。
3. 我把希望寄托在我们昨天得到的好消息上。
4. 这部影片是根据 D.H.劳伦斯的小说改编的。
5. 爱丽丝总是以事实为依据做出自己的判断。

Translation

IX. Translate the following sentences into Chinese.

1. This has saturated market demand, leaving the beneficiaries of the enrollment expansion in these specialties to confront job-hunting difficulties and a sense of loss.

2. An analysis of graduates' resumes has found that more than 80 percent of the resumes are deficient, often missing points that are essential for a resume.

3. The severe employment situation facing college graduates has drawn the attention of the government.

4. Employers are now shifting their focus from academic background to practical abilities of graduates.

5. Therefore, graduating students, though facing a severe situation, need not worry too much. However, they should adjust their mentality and employment concepts.

X. Translate the following sentences into English using the words or phrases in the brackets.

1. 我们所付出的所有努力结果都白费了。(result in)

2. 号召年轻人到基层单位,到不发达地区,到西部去工作。(call on)

3. 这情景使她心寒。(chill)

4. 在现代的语言学习中,学习者应该把重点放在语言的交际功能上,而不是语言的形式和结构上。(put/lay emphasis on sth)

5. 尽管他已在词典中查阅了这些新单词,但要准确翻译这篇文章还是有很大的困难。(have difficulty doing sth)

Part II Grammar

Tenses(时态)(四)

时态(四)完成进行时 (Perfect Continuous Tenses)

完成进行时是完成体与进行体的结合形式，表示动作在现在或过去某一时间以前开始，并延续到那个现在或过去的时间，而且有可能会继续进行下去。所表示的动作具有持续性、暂时性和未完成性。

1. 现在完成进行时 (Present Perfect Continuous Tense)

其构成形式如下：have/has been + V-ing. 它主要表示动作从过去某一时间开始一直延续到现在。现在这个动作可能已经完成，也可能仍然在进行当中，还会继续下去。如：

We have just been talking about you. 我们正谈你来着。(动作不再延续下去)

I have been waiting for you two hours. 我已经等了你2个小时了。(动作已经结束)

It has been snowing for the whole night. 雪已经下了整夜了。(有可能继续下去)

We have been learning Japanese for five years. 我们学日语已经5年时间了。(还会继续学)

此外,这个时态也可用以表示现在以前这段时间反复进行的动作：

I have been learning to play tennis for the past 2 months.
近两个月来我一直在学打网球。

We have been meeting each other quite a lot recently. 最近我们常常见面。

现在完成进行时只适用于动态动词，一些表示状态或五官感知的动词如 be, have, like, live, see, hear, know 等不能用于这一时态，而只能用现在完成时。如：

She has been ill for a long time. 她已病了好久了。

We have known each other since childhood. 我们从小就已认识了。

现在完成进行时与现在完成时在用法和表达的意义、功能方面有很大的相似之处,两种时态都可表示从过去某时开始并持续到说话时刻的动作,因而显得容易混淆,不易区分。在使用中需要注意以下几点:

现在完成进行时在多数情况下更强调动作的延续性,而现在完成时则表示动作到现在为止已经完成。

They have been widening the road. 他们正在拓宽马路。(正在进行)

They have widened the road. 他们把马路拓宽了。(已经完成)

现在完成进行时强调动作的直接结果;现在完成时则强调动作的最终结果。

I have finished the work. I can rest now. 工作完成了,我现在可以休息了。(强调最终结果)

You look so tired. What have you been doing? 你看上去很累,你做什么了?(强调直接结果)

2. 过去完成进行时 (Past Perfect Continuous Tense)

其构成形式如下:had been + V-ing。它的特点和用法与现在完成进行时基本相似,只是时间推移到了过去。它主要用来表示一个动作从过去某时开始,一直延续到另一个过去时刻,到那个时刻,该动作可能刚刚停止,也可能还在继续。如:

He had been teaching English for 45 years by the time he retired. 退休前,他教了45年的英语。(动作已经结束)

He told me that he had been waiting for me two hours. 他对我说他等了我2小时。(动作不再继续)

She had been studying since 6 o'clock. 她从6点钟开始就一直在学习。(动作可能继续)

It had been raining for two days. The fields were all under water. 已经下了两天的雨,地全都淹了。(动作可能还在进行)

过在完成进行时与过去完成时在用法上的区别类似于现在完成进行时与现在完成时的区别,前者强调动作的持续性和不间断性,后者更多是表示动作已停止,试比较:

Jenny had been studying 6 hours when her mother came back. 詹尼的母亲回来的时候,她已经学习了6个小时。(可能还会继续学习)

Jenny had studied 6 hours when her mother came back. 詹尼的母亲回来的时候,她已经学习了6个小时。(不再学习)

I. Complete the following sentences with the present/past perfect or the present/past perfect continuous.

1. I wonder if John _____ (forget) my number. I _____ (expect) him to call for the past two hours.

2. George _____ (collect) matchboxes ever since he left school. Now he _____ (collect) so many that he doesn't know where to put them.

3. Mrs. Brown _____ (live) next door for quite a long time now, but she _____ never _____ (say) more than "good morning" to me.

4. The fine tree _____ (stand) in the garden ever since I was a boy. I am glad they _____ (not cut) it down yet.

5. I _____ (ask) her to marry me for three years before we were engaged.

6. My mother was sewing a shirt. She _____ (sew) a lot of shirts before.

7. He'd better not drive. He _____ already _____ (drink) quite a lot.

8. He still couldn't sing although he _____ (take) lessons for years.

9. Peter _____ (be) a junior clerk for three years. Lately he _____ (look) for a better post but so far he _____ (not find) anything.

10. He _____ (read) in a bad light and her eyes were sore.

11. I _____ (write) the letter, so perhaps you would post it for me.

12. The mother took the children to the zoo yesterday. They _____ (want) to go for a long time.

13. That book _____ (lie) on your table for weeks. You _____ (not read) it yet.

14. She _____ (try) to learn how to swim for weeks, but she _____ (not succeed) yet.

II. Translate the following sentences into English, using perfect tenses.

1. 工作进行得怎么样了?
2. 都说这部电影非常感人,我一直盼望有机会去看一看。
3. 昨天晚上,我妈妈回来时,妹妹在床上一直哭了近半个小时。
4. 他爸爸从 1992 以来就当老师。
5. 他在这个村子已呆了一年的时间,一直在为他的研究收集真实的语言素材。
6. 到去年年底,他们已经治疗了五百多位病人。
7. 这些年来,我一直在为这家公司翻译资料。
8. 我向别人问过他的情况,没有人知道他那些年在做什么。
9. 我的自行车上周丢了,所以这些天来我一直走路上班。
10. 火整天都烧着,房间里十分暖和。

Part III Reading Practice

Guide to Reading

1. Words and Expressions to Learn

crash	adj.	done intensively to get quick results	突击式的,速成的
prompt	v.	cause or incite sb to do sth	促使,激励
enterprising	adj.	having courage and willingness	有事业心的,有进取心的
sideline	n.	occupation that is not one's main work	副业,兼职
legible	adj.	clear enough to be read easily	清楚的,易读的
blunt	adj.	frank, straightforward, not polite	直率的,不客气的
set about		begin a task, start doing sth	开始工作,着手做某事
look into		investigate, examine	调查,观察
come across		make an impression	给人以某种印象
depend on		be decided by, follow from sth	视……而定,取决于
stand out		much better than	远远超过,比……更好
cope with		deal with	对付,处理
apply for		request	申请,请求

2. *Pre-Reading Questions*

(1) Do you think it's important to write a curriculum vitae when you seek a job or apply for a position? Why?

(2) What should be included in a curriculum vitae?

Getting a Job

1   These days it's hard enough to find a chance to be interviewed, let alone get as far as a suitable job. Dozens of people every day **scour** (*v.* 搜寻) the Situations Vacant Columns of the press, send off their curriculum vitae or application form, and wait hopefully to be **summoned** (*v.* 召唤) for an interview. Now this, apparently, is where a lot of people fall down, because of their inadequacy at completing their application forms, according to Judith Davidson, author of *Getting a Job*, a book which has recently come on the market. This book, as the title suggests, is full of useful tips on how to set about finding yourself work in these difficult times. Our reporter, Christopher Shields, decided to look into this apparent inability of the British to sell themselves, and he spoke to Judith Davidson about it.

2   Judith: Very often a job application or curriculum vitae will contain basic grammatical or careless spelling mistakes, even from university graduates. Then those that do get as far as an interview become **inarticulate** (*adj.* 表达不清的) or **clumsy** (*adj.* 生硬的) when they try to talk about themselves. It doesn't matter how highly qualified or brilliant you may be, if you come across as tongue-tied and **gauche** (*adj.* 不善交际的), your chances of getting a job are pretty small.

3   Christopher: Judith Davidson lectures at a management training college for young men and women, most of whom have just graduated from university and gone there to take a crash course in management techniques. One of the hardest things is, not passing the course examinations successfully, but actually finding employment afterwards, so Judith now concentrates on helping trainees to set about doing just this.

4   Judith: Some letters are dirty and untidily written, with finger marks all over them and ink blots or even coffee stains. Others arrive on lined or flowered or

sometimes **scented** (*adj.* 有……香味的) paper—none of which is likely to make a good impression on the average business-like boss.

5   Christopher: This apparent inability of many people to make that initial impact on an employer by sending him an application which will stand out from the rest and persuade him you're the right one for the job prompted an enterprising young man, called Mark Ashworth, a recruitment consultant himself, to start writing job applications for other people for a fee, as a sideline. He told me he got the idea in America where it's already big business, and in the last few months alone he's written over 250 CVs. He feels that 80 percent of job applications received by personnel managers are inadequate in some way.

6   Mark: Many people simply can't cope with grammar and spelling and don't know what to put in, or leave out. Sometimes people **condense** (*v.* 简缩, 简述) their work experience so much that a future employer doesn't know enough about them. Then, on the other hand, some people go too far the other way. To give you an example, one CV I once received in my recruiting role was getting on for thirty pages long.

7   Christopher: Mark has an initial interview with all his **clients** (*n.* 委托人, 顾客) in which he tries to make them think about their **motivation** (*n.* 动机) and why they've done certain things in the past. He can often **exploit** (*v.* 利用, 开发) these experiences in the CV he writes for them, and show that they have been valuable preparation for the job now sought. He also believes that well-prepared job history and a good letter of application are absolutely essential.

8   Mark: Among the most important aspects of applications are spelling, correct grammar, content and **layout** (*n.* 布局, 安排). A new boss will probably also be impressed with a good reference or a letter of recommendation written by a former employer. The type of CV I aim to produce depends largely on the kind of job being applied for. They don't always have to be highly **sophisticated** (*adj.* 精细的, 精致的), but in certain cases this does help.

9   Christopher: Judith Davidson thought very much along the same lines as Mark. In her opinion, one of the most important aspects of job applications was that they should be easy to read.

10 Judith:… Many applicants send in letters and forms which are virtually unreadable. The essence of handwritten application is that they should be neat,

legible and the spelling should be accurate. I stress handwritten because most employers want a sample of their future employee's writing. Many believe this gives some indication of the character of the person who wrote it. Some people forget vital things like putting their own address or the date. Others fail to do what's required of them by a job advertisement.

11   Christopher: Judith believes that job seekers should always send an accompanying letter along with their application form stating clearly why their qualifications make them suitable for the vacancy.

12   Judith: Personal details have no place in letters of application. I well remember hearing about one such letter which stated, quite bluntly, I need more money to pay for my flat. No boss would be impressed by such directness.

13   Christopher: She added that the art of applying for jobs successfully was having to be learnt by more and more people these days, with the current unemployment situation. With as many as two or three hundred people applying for one vacancy, a boss would want to see only a small fraction of that number in person for an interview, so your application had to really outshine all the others to get you on the short list.

(813 words)

Exercises

Reading Comprehension

I. Read the following statements carefully, and decide whether they are true (T) or false (F) according to the passage.

1. Some people are at a loss what should be provided in an application. (　)
2. Applying for a job, one doesn't need at all a good reference or a letter of recommendation by a former boss. (　)
3. However highly qualified and brilliant an applicant is, he will be rejected, if he is tongue-tied and gauche during the interviews. (　)

4. An applicant's handwriting doesn't matter at all in a job application. (　)
5. Many applicants fail to get a job because of their own inability with application forms and CV. (　)
6. With hundreds of people fighting over one vacancy, one has to hire someone to write the application for him. (　)
7. When writing an application, we should make it as long as possible. (　)
8. This discussion mainly deals with how to please the employer. (　)

II. Translate into Chinese the following sentences taken from the passage.

1. This is where a lot of people fall down, because of their inadequacy at completing their application forms, according to Judith Davidson, author of *Getting a Job*, a book which has recently come on the market.
2. It doesn't matter how highly qualified or brilliant you may be, if you come across as tongue-tied and gauche, your chances of getting a job are pretty small.
3. This apparent inability of many people to make that initial impact on an employer by sending him an application which will stand out from the rest and persuade him you're the right one for the job prompted an enterprising young man, called Mark Ashworth, a recruitment consultant himself, to start writing job applications for other people for a fee, as a sideline.
4. Sometimes people condense their work experience so much that a future employer doesn't know enough about them. Then, on the other hand, some people go too far the other way.
5. With as many as two or three hundred people applying for one vacancy, a boss would want to see only a small fraction of that number in person for an interview, so your application had to really outshine all the others to get you on the short list.

III. Fill in the blanks with the words or phrases listed in Word and Expressions to Learn. Change the form where necessary.

1. He _____ well in the interview with his humorous response.
2. Although Claude was very busy, he still spared time taking the _____ course in spoken English.
3. If you want to get someone to do things for you, you should try to be polite, do

not ask _____.
4. The school authority must _____ finding solutions to the school's financial problems.
5. The teacher asked the students to write _____ when they were answering the questions.
6. She may not be the cleverest one, but she is most hard-working and _____.
7. Mrs. Rachel uses various classroom tasks to _____ her students to study.
8. Whether you can pass the exam or not _____ how hard you work.
9. He is a lawyer, and also teaches in that college as a _____.
10. He was murdered yesterday. The police are _____ the case.

Part IV Practical English

Personal Correspondences(私人信函)

私人信函一般指家人之间、师生之间等个人之间为进行信息交流、表达感情等而书写的往来信件。它的格式和语言不像公务信函那么正式，一般比较随便,语言平易、亲切而富有感情。

信的正文部分,可根据内容分段叙述。开头是寒暄语(Opening Sentences),中间部分叙述写信人的要求或写信目的(Body),结尾部分则是祝愿语(Closing Sentences)。

英文信封与中文信封的写法不同。习惯上,收信人的姓名、地址依次写在信封的中央。寄信人的姓名、地址写在信封的左上角。邮票贴在右上角。注意英文与中文地址的顺序也不同,应该是由小及大的顺序。如果是航空信(Air Mail)、挂号信(Registered)等,需要在信封的左下方注明。

1. 家信 (Family Letter)

Sample

Nov. 27, 2006

Dear Dad,

How's everything going on?

I am in a great quandary. To take them or not to take them! That is the question. Put the college board exams for the object, and my uncertain future for the reason for my indecision and you get a fair picture of my mental attitude. If I go to the University of Wisconsin, I do not need a record in examinations. There is no reason to go through the strain and stress of writing them; and I shall be perfectly happy at Wisconsin and certainly have excellent courses from which to choose, especially should I take history, science, or journalism. The historical library is second only to Harvard's, I understand, and the lecturers the finest to be found, all of them truly scientific historians. There is no place where one has more fun along with work than at Madison. I'll have a grand time there, Dad.

Then, on the other hand, I seem headed for the classics and modern language! I can specialize in that, too, at the University. And yet why have I studied so hard to prepare for the exams if I side-step them at the end? Do you think there is any likelihood of my going to Westminster? I'm glad I've studied to learn all this stuff. What shall I do?

　　　　　Please take care.

　　　　　　　　　　　　　　　　　　　　　　　　　Your loving daughter
　　　　　　　　　　　　　　　　　　　　　　　　　　　　Anita

亲爱的爸爸：

　　家中一切可好？

　　我现在非常困惑。参加考试或不参加考试，这是一个问题。考大学和不能确定的未来使我无所适从，你可以看出我心情不定的情形了。如果我到威斯康星大学，我是不需要考试成绩的，我又何必费心应付考试呢。我在威斯康星将会很快乐而且可选择最喜欢的课程，尤其是历史、科学或新闻学。我知道那儿的历史图书馆仅次于哈佛大学，而且那里的老师是最好的，他们都是科学的"历史学家"。没有哪个地方能比麦迪逊再好的了，那儿有工作又好玩。爸爸，我在那里将会是非常快乐的。

　　另外，我好像长于古典文学或语文。在威斯康星大学我可以专攻这一方面。如果我最终可以逃避考试，那么我为什么要很辛苦去准备它们呢？您认为我有去威斯敏斯特的可能性吗？很高兴我已经学会了去了解这一切。我将要怎么办呢？

　　望保重。

　　　　　　　　　　　　　　　　　　　　　　　　您亲爱的女儿
　　　　　　　　　　　　　　　　　　　　　　　　安妮塔
　　　　　　　　　　　　　　　　　　　　　　　　2006 年 11 月 27 日

　　　　　　　　　　　　　　　Stamp

Anita Smith
924 W 32nd St.
Chicago, IL 60618

　　　　　　　　　　　Mr. John Smith
　　　　　　　　　　　88 Main Street
　　　　　　　　　　　Bakersfield, CA 95822

Air Mail

2. 约会信 (Date Letter)

Sample

Dec. 10, 2006

Dear Miss Smith,

  How are you? Excuse me for my long silence.

  My brother Peter will be staying with us for a few days during the Christmas holidays and my wife and I have planned a family dinner for him next Saturday evening at seven o'clock so that he can meet some of our friends. We should be delighted if you could join us. I hope you will let me know that you can come.

  Please remember me to John.

Yours Sincerely,
Arthur

亲爱的史密斯小姐：

  你好，原谅我好久没有写信了。

  我的弟弟彼得将在圣诞假期期间到我们家小住几日，我和妻子计划在下星期六晚7时在家中为他设便宴，以便他可以和我们的一些朋友见面。若您能出席，我们会感到很高兴，希望您能告诉我您能来。

  请代我向约翰问好。

诚挚的
阿瑟
2006年12月10日

Useful Expressions

It was a pleasure to receive your letter of the 5th of October.
很高兴收到您10月5号的来信。

I wish to say how pleased we were to receive your letter.

想告诉您我们收到您的来信是多么高兴。

Your wonderful letter came this morning.

你精彩的信今天早上寄到。

How are you? Excuse me for my long silence.

你好,原谅我许久没有写信了。

How time flies!

时间过得真快!

Useful Endings

Warm regards and best wishes.

谨致以亲切的问候及良好的祝愿。

Please remember me to John.

请代我向约翰问好。

If there is anything further that I can do for you, please don't hesitate to ask.

如果还有什么事情我可以为您做,请不要客气。

Write soon.

请速回信。

Forgive me for making this so short, I'll write more soon.

请原谅此函简短,我不久会再写信的。

Please take care.

请保重身体。

Complete the following letter according to the Chinese version.

亲爱的丽莎：
　　昨天收到了你的来信，谢谢！
　　很高兴得知今年夏天你要到中国来。你说要呆一个月，我希望你能过来看看我们。
　　我们有一空房间，你住我家没问题，你想住多久就可以住多久。今年夏天我们不打算出游，因此时间安排也没问题。
　　请尽快回信并告知是否能来。祝你和你的家人快乐！
　　　　　　　　　　　　　　　　爱你的
　　　　　　　　　　　　　　　　海伦
　　　　　　　　　　　　　　　2006年4月30日

April 30th, 2006

Dear Lisa,

　　Thanks so much for your letter, _____ (1) arrived yesterday.

　　I'm very _____ (2) to hear you are coming to China this summer. You say that your holiday will _____ (3) a month, so I hope that you will be able to come and see us.

　　We have a spare room, so there is no problem about putting you _____ (4) and you are welcome to stay for as long as you like. We are not going away this summer, so there is no problem about arranging dates.

　　Please write soon and tell me if you can come. My best wishes _____ (5) you and your family.

　　　　　　　　　　　　　　　　Love
　　　　　　　　　　　　　　　　Helen

Part V English Salon

No Problem

A bald man took a seat in a beauty shop. "How can I help you?" asked the stylist. "I went for a hair transplant," the guy explained, "but I couldn't stand the pain. If you can make my hair look like yours without causing me any discomfort, I'll pay you $5,000."

"No problem," said the stylist, and he quickly shaved his head.

Can you find where the joke comes in?

Unit Four

Part I TEXT

Guide to Text-Learning

1. Words and Expressions Related to the Topic

disabled	残废的
disability	残废
injure	伤害
beauty	美人
optimistic	乐观的
pessimistic	悲观的
on one's own	独立地
confident	自信的
broken in health but not in spirit	身残志不残

2. Grammatical Structures to Learn

(1) I walked **with my face looking at the floor** so people would not see the ugly me.

我低着头走路不让人们看到我很丑的样子。

(2) I grew up imagining that everyone looked at me with disdain, **as if** my appearance were my fault.

在我成长的过程中,我总是想象着每个人都鄙视地看着我,就好像我的外貌是我的过错似的。

Warm-Up Questions:

1. Do you know the story about Zhang Haidi?
2. How do you think about the spirit of this story?
3. If you were disabled, what would you do in your future life?

Hold Your Head up High

1   I was fifteen months old, a happy **carefree** kid until the day I fell. It was a bad fall. I landed on a glass rabbit which cut my eye badly enough to blind it. Trying to save the eye, the doctors **stitched** the eyeball together where it was cut, leaving a big ugly scar in the middle of my eye. The attempt failed, but my mama, in all of her **wisdom**, found a doctor who knew that if the eye were removed entirely, my face would grow up badly **distorted**, so my scarred, **sightless**, cloudy and gray eye lived on with me. And as I grew, this sightless eye in so many ways controlled me.

2   I walked with my face looking at the floor so people would not see the ugly me. Sometimes people, even strangers, asked me **embarrassing** questions or made hurtful remarks. When the kids played games, I was always the "monster." I grew up imagining that everyone looked at me with **disdain**, as if my **appearance** were my fault. I always felt like I was **abnormal**.

3   Yet Mama would say to me, at every

---

carefree /ˈkeəfriː/ *adj.*
without responsibilities or worries; cheerful
无忧无虑的，快乐的

stitch /stitʃ/ *v.*
sew
缝合

wisdom /ˈwizdəm/ *n.*
quality of being wise
智慧

distort /disˈtɔːt/ *v.*
pull or twist sth out of its usual shape; misrepresent
使(某物)变形，扭曲；曲解

sightless /ˈsaitlis/ *adj.*
unable to see; blind
看不见的，失明的

embarrassing /imˈbærəsiŋ/ *adj.*
making sb feel awkward or ashamed
令人困窘的，令人难堪的

disdain /disˈdein/ *n.*
a feeling or show of contempt and aloofness; scorn
轻视，蔑视

appearance /əˈpiərəns/ *n.*
what sb or sth appears to be; the thing which shows
外表，外貌，外观

abnormal /æbˈnɔːməl/ *adj.*
not typical, usual, or regular; not normal
反常的，变态的，不正常的

turn, "Hold your head up high and face the world." It became a belief that I relied on. She had started when I was young. She would hold me in her arms and **stroke** my hair and say, "If you hold your head up high, it will be okay, and people will see your beautiful soul." She continued this message whenever I wanted to hide.

4   Those words have meant different things to me over the years. As a little child, I thought Mama meant, "Be careful or you will fall down or bump into something because you are not looking." As a youth, even though I **tended** to look down to hide my shame, I found that sometimes when I held my head up high and let people know me, they liked me. My mama's words helped me begin to realize that by letting people look at my face, I let them recognize the **intelligence** and beauty behind both eyes even if they couldn't see it on the surface.

5   In high school I was successful both academically and socially. I was even elected class president, but on the inside I still felt like an abnormal person. All I really wanted was to look like everyone else. When things got really bad, I would cry to my mama and she would look at me with loving eyes and say, "Hold your head up high and face the world. Let them see the beauty that is inside."

6   When I met the man who became my partner for life, we looked each other straight in the eye, and he told me I was beautiful inside and out. He meant it. My mama's love and **encouragement** was the spark that gave me the **confidence** to overcome my own doubt. I had faced **misfortune**, **encountered** many problems and learned not only to **appreciate** myself but to have deep **compassion** for others.

7   "Hold your head up high," has been heard many times in my home. Each of

---

stroke /strəuk/ v.
pass the hand gently over a surface, usu. again and again
(用手)轻抚(某物表面)

tend /tend/ v.
be inclined to move; have a direction
倾向,有某种趋势,趋于

intelligence /in'telidʒəns/ n.
capacity to acquire and apply knowledge
才智;学习和应用知识的能力

encouragement /in'kʌridʒmənt/ n.
action of encouraging; thing that encourages
鼓励,支持,激励,促进(的事物)

confidence /'kɔnfidəns/ n.
belief in oneself or others
信心,信任

misfortune /mis'fɔːtʃən/ n.
bad luck; unfortunate condition, accident or event
不幸,灾祸,不幸事故

encounter /in'kauntə/ v.
meet, especially unexpectedly; come upon
不期而遇,偶然遇见

appreciate /ə'priːʃieit/ v.
judge rightly the value of; understand and enjoy
正确地判断……的价值;鉴赏;重视

compassion /kəm'pæʃən/ n.
pity; feeling for the sufferings of others, prompting one to give help
同情,怜悯

my children has felt its **invitation**. The gift my mama gave me lives on in another **generation**.

(540 words)

> **invitation** /ˌinviˈteiʃən/ n.
> thing that tempts or encourages sb to do sth
> 鼓励，激励；引诱的事物
>
> **generation** /ˌdʒenəˈreiʃən/ n.
> single stage in a family history
> （家史中的）一代

Phrases and Useful Expressions

in so many ways	in so many aspects	在许多方面；以多种方式
as if/as though	in the same way that it would be if	似乎，好像，仿佛
rely on	count on or depend on sb/sth	依赖，指望
fall down	stop standing suddenly; collapse	跌倒，倒下；倒塌
bump into sth/sb	knock or strike sth with a dull-sounding blow; meet sb by chance	撞到；巧遇
hold sth/sb up	obstruct or delay; offer or present as an example	阻挠或延迟；举……为例
live on	continue to live or exist	继续生活或存在

Notes

1. Trying to save the eye, the doctors stitched the eyeball together where it was cut, leaving a big ugly scar in the middle of my eye. 为了挽救我的眼睛，医生们缝合了我眼球上的伤口。从此，在我的眼睛中间留下了难看的疤痕。

本句中"trying"和"leaving"两个现在分词分别在句中作状语，它们的逻辑主语就是 the doctors。

我们还可以看下面的两个例子：

Sitting at the back of the classroom, we can't hear a word.

Inspired by what he said, we are beginning to show an interest in English.

2 I walked with my face looking at the floor so people would not see the ugly me. 我低着头走路不让人们看到我很丑的样子。

本句中介词 with 后接复合宾语构成介词短语，在句中作伴随状语。

表示否定意义时可用 without 引导，如：

The war was over without a shot being fired. 没开一枪，这次战争就结束了。

3 ... if the eye were removed entirely, my face would grow up badly distorted. 如果我的眼睛被完全摘除掉，我的脸将会扭曲。

本句运用了虚拟语气(Subjunctive Mood)表示假设的情况。在虚拟语气中，从句中的 be 动词，无论主语是什么人称，都用 were，而主句用 would/should/could+ 动词原形的结构，如下面的例子：

If I were a student now, I would study English hard.

4 I grew up imagining that everyone looked at me with disdain, as if my appearance were my fault. 在我成长的过程中，我总是想象着每个人都鄙视地看着我，就好像我的外貌是我的过错似的。

本句中 as if 引导的状语从句在特定语境可用虚拟语气。

Reading Aloud and Memorizing the Following

I. Read the following paragraph taken from the text until you learn it by heart.

When I met the man who became my partner for life, we looked each other straight in the eye, and he told me I was beautiful inside and out. He meant it. My mama's love and encouragement were the spark that gave me the confidence to overcome my own doubt. I had faced misfortune, encountered many problems, and learned not only to appreciate myself but to have deep compassion for others.

Comprehension of the text.

II. Choose the best answer to each of the following questions according to the passage.

1. What can we learn from this text?
   A. We should face any difficulties with our courage.
   B. Beautiful soul is much more important than beautiful appearance.
   C. We should be confident in overcoming any troubles.
   D. We should not spend time making up ourselves.
2. Why was there an ugly scar in the middle of the author's eye?
   A. Because the author was so naughty that she fell while she was playing.
   B. Because the author had hurt herself when she played with my friends.
   C. Because the author's eye was hurt by a glass rabbit, and the doctor had to stitch the eyeball together where it was cut.
   D. The author had an unsuccessful operation on her eyes because of her eyesight.
3. What does "hold your head up high" mean in the text?
   A. Be careful to fall down or bump into something.
   B. Be self-confident and make people see your beautiful soul.
   C. Be proud of the job you are doing.
   D. Looking down upon anybody to show your beauty.
4. How was the author doing in her high school?
   A. She was successful both academically and socially.
   B. She could not get on well with her classmates.
   C. All of her classmates were tired of the author and did not want to study with her.
   D. She could not catch up with her study.
5. What did the author really get from her mother's words?
   A. The author was the most beautiful girl in the world.
   B. The author should not only appreciate herself but also have deep compassion for others.

C. The author should be careful not to fall down and hurt her eyes again.

D. The author should respect her parents and other people who cared about her.

III. Answer the following questions with the information you've got from the text.

1. How did the author hurt her eye badly? (Para.1)
2. What did the author feel like about her ugly appearance? (Para. 2)
3. What did the author's mother say to her? (Para. 3)
4. What did her mother's words mean to the author when she was a child and when she was a youth? (Para. 4)
5. Do you think the author really understand what her mother said?

Vocabulary

IV. Spell out the words with the help of the given definitions and the first letters.

1. misrepresent (d _____)
2. causing sb to feel awkward or ashamed (e _____)
3. blind (s _____)
4. experience and knowledge shown in making decisions and judgments (w _____)
5. different from what is normal, ordinary or expected (a _____)
6. pass the hand gently over a surface again and again (s _____)
7. be likely to behave in a certain way or to have a certain characteristic or influence (t _____)
8. power of learning, understanding and reasoning (i _____)
9. belief that one is right or that one is able to do sth (c _____)
10. unfortunate accident or happenings (m _____)

V. Fill in the blanks with the words given below. Change the form where necessary.

sight	wise	abnormal	intelligent	confident
appreciate	tend	appear	embarrass	encourage

1. The teacher's words were a great _____ to him.

2. He couldn't answer the _____ question.
3. I was entirely cheated by her _____.
4. Women _____ to live longer than men.
5. You can't fully _____ foreign literature in translation.
6. I have little _____ in him.
7. I have nothing special. I'm just a person of average _____.
8. We have suffered a lot from the _____ weather conditions.
9. She had acquired much _____ during her long life.
10. Her eyes were badly hurt in the fall and they became _____.

VI. Fill in the blanks with proper prepositions or adverbs.

1. There is a pain _____ the middle of his back.
2. My grandmother lived _____ for many years after my grandfather died.
3. My younger brother always dreams to become a scientist when he grows _____.
4. Hold your head up _____ and you can overcome any difficulties.
5. Mary was so careless that she fell _____ and hurt her leg.
6. When my mother told stories to me, she always looked _____ me with a smile.
7. _____ a college student, I should take part in some instructive activities.
8. He made me laugh _____ telling me funny stories.
9. Each _____ us has a good time in the travel to Beijing.
10. In the dark I bumped _____ a chair by the window.

Structure

VII. Rewrite the following sentences after the models.

Model 1 I walked. **My face looked at the floor.**

I walked **with my face looking at the floor.**

1. The teacher went into the classroom. The students followed him.
2. He fell asleep. The lamp burned.

3. The sale usually takes place outside the house. The audience sits on benches, chairs or boxes.
4. The teacher came in. His hand carried a book.
5. The President visited our college. The bodyguard stood around.

> **Model 2**
> I learned **to** appreciate myself.
> I learned **to** have deep compassions for others.
> I learned **not only to** appreciate myself **but to** have deep compassion for others.

1. Jack studies English well.
   He helps others with their English.
2. The students are required to attend the meeting.
   The teachers are required to attend the meeting.
3. She is interested in the subject.
   All her students are beginning to show an interest in it.
4. He likes reading fiction.
   He likes reading poetry.
5. My summer's work proved to be interesting.
   My summer's work proved to be instructive.

VIII. *Study the model and complete the following sentences, by using the conjunction "as if."*

> **Model** I grew up imagining that everyone looked at me with disdain, <u>as if my appearance were my fault</u>. (好像我的外貌是我的过错似的)

1. She looked pale _____. (好像看到了鬼似的)
2. He waved his arms _____. (像鸟一样地)
3. The electric current flows through a conductor _____. (好像液体般地)
4. He spoke to me _____. (好像我是聋子似的)
5. You speak _____. (好像你真的去过那里一样)

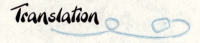

IX. Translate the following sentences into Chinese.

1. I walked with my face looking at the floor so people would not see the ugly me.

2. If you hold your head up high, it will be okay, and people will see your beautiful soul.

3. My mama's words helped me begin to realize that by letting people look at my face, I let them recognize the intelligence and beauty behind both eyes even if they couldn't see it on the surface.

4. When I met the man who became my partner for life, we looked each other straight in the eye, and he told me I was beautiful inside and out.

5. My mama's love and encouragement were the spark that gave me the confidence to overcome my own doubt.

X. Translate the following sentences into English using the words or phrases in the brackets.

1. 南希在许多方面比她姐姐强得多。(in so many ways)

2. 现在人们依赖计算机工作。(rely on)

3. 我在冬天经常睡得较早。(tend to do)

4. 莫扎特虽已作古,但他的音乐作品却万古流芳。(live on)

5. 即使一路要走着去,我也要走到那里。(even though)

Part II Grammar

Passive Voice(被动语态)(一)

语态(Voice)是表示主语和动词之间语法和语义关系的动词形式。英语动词有主动语态和被动语态。当主语是动作的发出者时，动词用主动语态(Active Voice)；当主语是动作的承受者时，动词要用被动语态(Passive Voice)。只有及物动词才有被动语态。如：

Scientists **have been puzzled** for decades by how turtles manage to navigate across the Atlantic—but now they **know**.

几十年来，科学家一直对海龟如何能穿越大西洋迷惑不解——但现在他们知道了。

这句话中，scientist 是 puzzle 的承受者，故 puzzle 用被动语态。they 是 know 的发出者，故 know 用主动语态。

1. 被动语态的结构形式

动词的被动语态是由助动词 be 加动词的过去分词构成的。助动词 be 无词义，随主语的人称、数和时态等的不同形式而变化。主动语态的句子结构与被动语态的句子结构如下所示：

主动语态：

动作的发出者 + 主动语态 + 动作的承受者

主语	谓语	宾语
They	have put off	the meeting.
他们	已经推迟了	会议。

被动语态：

动作的承受者 + 被动语态(be + V-ed) + (by + 动作的发出者)

主语	谓语	by 短语引出动作的发出者(状语)
She	is liked	by all of us.
她	受到我们所有人的喜爱。	

2. 被动语态的各种时态

下面以 make 为例,说明不同时态的被动语态形式:

现在范畴	一般现在时	am / is / are made
	现在进行时	am / is / are being made
	现在完成时	has / have been made
过去范畴	一般过去时	was / were made
	过去进行时	was / were/ being made
	过去完成时	had been made
将来范畴	一般将来时	shall / will be made
	将来完成时	shall / will have been made

完成进行时态一般不用被动语态。

e.g. Such books **are written** for middle school students.

这种书是为中学生写的。

e.g. It **is said** that the police will look into the matter.

据说警方将调查此事。

e.g. This question **is being discussed** at the meeting.

会上正在讨论这个问题。

e.g. The car **was** seriously **damaged**.

汽车受到了严重的损坏。

e.g. Three people **have** so far **been killed** in the storms sweeping across the north of England and southern Scotland.

在席卷英格兰北部和苏格兰南部的暴风雨中,已有三人丧生。

e.g. A short play **will be put on** by them at the party.

他们将要在晚会上演出一个短剧。

Exercises

I. Turn the following sentences into passive voice.

1. Someone burned down the Houses of Parliament.
2. They will invite you to the dinner, too.
3. They will have completed the bridge by the end of this month.

4. The police have caught the murderer.

5. The mechanic is examining the engine of the car.

6. They had loaded the truck with sand.

7. They were building a bridge.

8. The lady cleans the rooms every day.

9. I haven't written a card.

10. His teacher is helping him with his English.

II. Complete each of the following sentences with the most appropriate word or words from the four choices marked A, B, C and D.

1. Harvard University, which _____ in 1836, is one of the oldest universities in the United States of America.

    A. found   B. founded   C. was found   D. was founded

2. If one _____ by pride, he will reject useful advice and friendly assistance.

    A. overcomes   B. is overcome
    C. has been overcome D. overcame

3. The goods _____ when we arrived at the airport.

    A. were just unloading   B. were just being unloaded
    C. had just unloaded   D. had just been unloaded

4. Each child _____ an apple at the end of yesterday's party.

    A. has been offered   B. were offered
    C. was offered   D. has offered

5. It was not until man had learned how to make iron and steel that the construction of various machines _____ possible.

    A. were made   B. had made
    C. made   D. was made

6. Tom _____ as the best student in his class.

    A. regards   B. regarded   C. has regarded   D. is regarded

7. The sports meeting _____ because of the bad weather.

    A. put off   B. was put off   C. was putted off   D. has put off

8. Look! The flag is _____ now.

    A. being raised   B. being rose
    C. risen   D. raising

9. All the machines _____ by the end of the following week.
   A. were repaired   B. would be repaired
   C. will have been repaired D. were being repaired
10. My pictures _____ until next week.
    A. won't develop   B. aren't developing
    C. don't develop   D. won't be developed

Part III Reading Practice

Guide to Reading

1. **Words and Expressions to Learn**

positive	showing confidence and optimism	自信的,乐观的;建设性的
curious	eager to know or learn	富于好奇心的;感兴趣的
complain	say that one is dissatisfied, unhappy	抱怨,埋怨
react	respond	回应,做出反应
reflect	think deeply about; consider	沉思或追忆(往事),思考
consciousness	state or condition of being conscious	知觉,意识;觉悟
point out	direct attention to sth	指出(使注意某事)
cut away	remove sth by cutting	切除,剪去
go through	experience, endure or suffer sth	经历;忍受;遭遇
take action	do sth in response to what has happened	采取行动,行动起来
thanks to	owing to; because of	因为,由于

2. *Pre-Reading Questions:*

(1) Many people say that happiness depends on one's life attitude, what do you think about it?

(2) What factors are important to happiness? Discuss this question with your classmates.

Life Is Full of Choices

1   Michael is the kind of guy you love to hate. He is always **in a good mood** (心情很好) and always has something positive to say. When someone asked him how he was doing, he would reply, "If I were any better, I'd be twins!" He was a natural **motivator** (积极分子).

2   If an employee was having a bad day, Michael was there telling the employee how to look on the positive side of the situation. Seeing this style really made me curious, so one day I went up to Michael and asked him, "I don't get it. You can't be positive all the time. How do you do it?" Michael replied, "Each morning I wake up and say to myself, 'Mike, you have two choices today. You can choose to be in a good mood or you can choose to be in a bad mood.' I choose to be in a good mood. Each time something bad happens, I can choose to be a **victim** (n. 受害者) or choose to learn from it. I choose to learn from it. Every time someone comes to me complaining, I can choose to accept complaining or I can point out the positive side of life. I choose the positive side of life."

3   "Yeah, right. It isn't that easy." I protested.

4   "Yes, it is," Michael said. "Life is all about choices. When you cut away all the junk, every situation is a choice. You choose how you react to situations. You choose how people will affect your mood. You choose to be in a good mood or bad mood. The bottom line is: It's your choice how you live life." I reflected on what Michael said.

5   Soon **thereafter** (adv. 此后), I left the big **enterprise** (n. 企业, 公司) that I had worked in for years to start my own business. We lost touch, but I often thought about him when I made a choice about life instead of reacting to it. Several years later, I heard Michael was involved in a serious accident, falling off 60 feet from a communications tower.

6   After 18 hours of **surgery** (n. 手术) and weeks of **intensive care** (细心照料), Michael was released from the hospital with rods placed in his back. I saw Michael about six months after the accident. When I asked him how he was, he replied, "If I were any better, I'd be twins. Want to see my scars?" I **declined** (v. 谢绝) to see his

wounds, but did ask him what had gone through his mind as the accident took place.

7 "The first thing that went through my mind was the well being of my soon-to-born (即将出世的) daughter," Michael replied. "Then, as I lay on the ground, I remembered had two choices: I could choose to live or I could choose to die. I choose to live."

8 "Weren't you scared? Did you lose consciousness?" I asked.

9 Michael continued, "The nursing staffs were great. They kept telling me I was going to be fine. But when they wheeled me into the operation room and I saw the expressions on the faces of the doctors and nurses, I got really scared. In their eyes, l read 'He's a dead man.' I knew I needed to take action." "What did you do?" I asked. "Well, there was a big **burly** (*adj.* 健壮的) nurse shouting questions at me," said Michael. "She asked me if I was **allergic** (*adj.* 由过敏引起的) to anything. 'Yes,' I said. The doctors and nurses stopped working as they waited for my reply. I took a deep breath and **yelled** (*v.* 喊叫), 'Gravity.' Over their laughter, I told them, 'I'm choosing to live. Operate on me as if I am alive, not dead.'"

10 Michael lived, thanks to the skill of his doctors, but also because of his amazing attitude. I learned from him that every day we have a choice to live fully. Attitude is everything.

(632 words)

Reading Comprehension

I. Read the following statements carefully, and decide whether they are true (T) or false (F) according to the passage.

1. Michael was always in a good mood and had nothing to worry about. (   )

2. Michael always encouraged people to look on the positive side of the situation. (   )

3. The author could understand why Michael was always in a good mood at first. (   )

4. The author left the big company he worked for years because he was fired. (   )
5. Michael fell off 60 feet from a communications tower and lost consciousness. (   )
6. In the hospital, Michael wasn't scared and wanted to stay alive. (   )
7. The doctors and the nurses in the hospital thought it possible to save his life and encourage him to be confident. (   )
8. One's attitude towards the situation is very important. (   )

II. Translate into Chinese the following sentences taken from the passage.

1. If an employee was having a bad day, Michael was there telling the employee how to look on the positive side of the situation.
2. Each time something bad happens, I can choose to be a victim or choose to learn from it. I choose to learn from it.
3. Soon thereafter, I left the big enterprise that I had worked in for years to start my own business.
4. I declined to see his wounds, but did ask him what had gone through his mind as the accident took place.
5. Michael lived, thanks to the skill of his doctors, but also because of his amazing attitude.

III. Fill in the blanks with the words or phrases listed in Word and Expressions to Learn. Change the form where necessary.

1. I need time to _____ on your offer.
2. All the members _____ positively to the suggestion.
3. The blow caused him to lose _____.
4. They _____ all the dead branches from the tree.
5. All the people must _____ to stop the fire spreading.
6. _____ your help, we finished the design ahead of time.
7. The professor _____ several mistakes in the composition.
8. He is always _____ about the bad weather in Chengdu.
9. Michael suggested that everyone should try to be _____ in dealing with the problem.
10. He is a _____ boy who is always asking questions.

Part IV Practical English

Business Correspondences(业务信函)(一)

英文书信可分为私人信函和业务信函两大类。私人信函所包含的项目比业务信函少些,语言也更加通俗随意。业务信函主要由六部分构成。

1. 信头(Heading/Letterhead):包括写信人的地址、邮政编码、电话、传真号码及电子邮件地址(Writer's e-mail address)等和写信日期(Date)。私人信函中一般没有信头;公司业务信函用纸上一般印有信头,不必另行再写。信头要写在信件的右上方。
2. 收信人的姓名与地址(Inside Name and Address):在信头下方,位置靠左边。私人信函中无此部分。
3. 称呼(Salutation):如知道对方姓名,可用 Dear 加名字,也可用 Dear 加称呼和姓氏。不知道对方姓名时,可用 Dear Sir, Dear Sirs, 或 Gentlemen, Ladies。称呼的位置在信内地址下面。
4. 正文(Body of the Letter):信的主体,要求开门见山,简明扼要,条理清楚。
5. 结束语(Complimentary Close):在正文下面,只占一行,一般为 Yours sincerely/ truly/faithfully, 也可把 yours 放在后面,写成 Sincerely yours 等。
6. 署名(Signature):署名要用手写。

1. Letter of Invitation

Sample

College of Foreign Languages and Cultures
Sichuan University
17 Binjiang Road, Chengdu 610000
Tel. 028-86557365   Fax 028-86337986
http://flc.scu.edu.cn/cofl/col2101.asp

August 15, 2006

Dear Professor Parley:

  It would give me great pleasure to have your presence at a meeting of English Language teaching scheduled for September the sixth, 2006 at the College of Foreign Languages and Cultures of Sichuan University to discuss various problems in English language teaching.

  Your thinking on the subject would contribute greatly to the success of the conference. Do let me know if you can make it.

Cordially,

(Signature)

Li Ping, Dean of the College

四川大学外国语学院

成都市滨江路 17 号 610000

电话:028-86557365　传真:028-86337986

网址:http://flc.scu.edu.cn/cofl/col2101.asp

尊敬的帕利教授:

  我们非常荣幸地邀请您出席于 2006 年 9 月 6 日在四川大学外国语学院举行的英语教学会议,探讨英语教学存在的各种问题。

  您对这一专题的看法将对此次会议的成功起到很大作用。请通知我们您能否到会。

您诚挚的

(签名)

学院院长:李 平

2006 年 8 月 15 日

2. Accepting a conference invitation

Sample

Dear Mr. Li:

   Thank you for your invitation to attend the meeting of English language teaching to be held at the College of Foreign Languages and Cultures of Sichuan University, September the sixth, 2006.

   I am happy to be there and look forward to it with pleasure.

Cordially,
(Signature)
Parley

尊敬的李先生：

   感谢您邀请我参加 2006 年 9 月 6 日于四川大学外国语学院举行的英语教学会议。

   我很愿意出席并期待这一时刻的到来。

您诚挚的
（签名）
帕利

3. Apologizing for being unable to accept a conference invitation

Sample

Dear Mr. Li:

   Thank you for your invitation to attend the meeting of English language teaching to be held at the College of Foreign Languages and Cultures of Sichuan University, September the sixth, 2006. I had hoped that it would be possible for me to be there, but now I find the rush of business makes it impractical.

   Please accept my regrets, and I'll try to make it next time.

Cordially,
(Signature)
Parley

尊敬的李先生：

　　感谢您邀请我参加2006年9月6日于四川大学外国语学院举行的英语教学会议。起初我希望能够出席此次会议,但现在发现公务繁忙,故不能到会。

　　未能出席,深表歉意,我争取下次参加。

您诚挚的
（签名）
帕利

常用套语：

1. Thank you a thousand times for your invitation.

   非常感谢你的邀请。

2. I shall be very happy to accept your kind invitation to speak at the meeting.

   我非常乐意接受你的邀请并在会上讲话。

3. Thank you for your invitation to attend the Press Conference to be held in the City Hall, June the first, 2004. I'm happy to have our company represented.

   感谢您邀请我参加2004年6月1日在市政厅举行的记者招待会。我很愿意代表我们公司出席这次会议。

4. Luckily, I have no other plans for the date you mentioned, and shall be happy to see you at 6 at the City Hall.

   幸运的是,我在那天没有别的安排,很愿意6点钟与您在市政厅见面。

5. It was thoughtful of you to invite me, and I am extremely sorry I cannot accept. I do hope you will ask me again some time!

   承蒙您热情相邀,恰巧因故不能前往,深表歉意。但愿以后能再次得到您的邀请。

6. Unfortunately, I have other plans for the date you mentioned, but shall be happy to make a date for some other convenient time.

   很遗憾,由于有其他事务安排,所以无法赴约。我很愿意在以后方便的时候前去拜会。

7. Please accept my regrets, and I'll try to make it next year.

   未能出席,深表歉意。我争取明年参加。

Writing Practice

Complete the following Letter of Invitation according to the Chinese version.

尊敬的约翰·史密斯先生：
　　我们非常荣幸地邀请贵公司参加于 8 月 29 日到 9 月 4 日在我中心举办的 2007 年国际商品交易会，关于交易会的详情我们一周内将寄给您。希望不久能收到您的回复，并能来参加。

　　　　　　　　　　　　　您诚挚的
　　　　　　　　　　　　　（签名）
　　　　　　　　　　　　　大卫·布朗

Dear Mr. John Smith:

　　We are honored to ＿＿ (1)　your Corporation to attend the 2007 International Fair which ＿＿ (2)　from August 29 to September 4 at our Center. Full ＿＿ (3) on the Fair will be sent in a week.

　　We look forward to ＿＿ (4) soon, and hope that you ＿＿ (5) to attend.

　　　　　　　　　　　　　Yours faithfully,
　　　　　　　　　　　　　(Signature)
　　　　　　　　　　　　　David Brown

Part V English Salon

Silly Questions with Clever Answers

1. When is a man's pocket empty and yet has something in it?
2. Who dares sit before the Queen with his hat on?
3. Why do we buy clothes?
4. What breaks but never falls, and what falls but never breaks?
5. Why is a river so rich?

Try to get the answers to the above questions.

Unit Five

Part I TEXT

Guide to Text-Learning

1. Words and Expressions Related to the Topic

commitmen	义务,责任
appreciation	欣赏,赏识
quantity	数量
anticipate	预期
fault-finding	挑毛病;找茬
belittle	贬损;轻视
negative	消极的,负面的
surmount	克服
larynx	喉(管)
therapist	(精神)治疗专家
explore	探索;勘察
acid sarcasm	尖酸刻薄的话;讽刺挖苦的话
fall apart	崩溃;坍塌;倒下

2. Grammatical Structures to Learn

   (1) **I remind** him **of** the three (sales) he made last week.
   我提醒他说他上周做成了三笔生意。

   (2) One of the tools these families identified as necessary for **coping with** crisis is adaptability.
   解决家庭矛盾的有效方法之一就是不断调整自我,做出某些改变。

   (3) He **set aside** time for his family.
   他抽出时间来照顾家庭。

Warming-Up Questions:

1. What is family?
2. Why is a strong family so important?
3. What should we do to build up a strong family?

Secrets of Strong Families

1   Do strong families still exist? The answer is Yes. According to the Family Strengths Research Project, the key qualities for making a strong family **function** are:

2   **COMMITMENT**

3   **Crucial** to any family's success is an investment of time, energy, **spirit** and heart, an investment **otherwise** known as commitment.

4   Some families have seen commitment **eroded** by a more **subtle** enemy—work, and its demand on time, attention and energy. One father offered this **insight**: "Sometimes I feel that the time I spend with my sons could be better spent at the office. Then I remind myself that the **productivity** report will affect life for a few days or weeks. I must do it and it's important, but my job as a father is more important."

5   "If I'm a good father to my sons, they're likely to be good parents too. Someday—after I'm gone, and certainly after that report has **rotted**—my grandchild or great-grandchild will have a good father because I was a good

---

function /'fʌŋkʃən/ v.
operate; act
运行；发挥作用
crucial /'kruːʃəl/ adj.
decisive; critical; fundamental
有决定性的；极重要的；根本的
spirit /'spirit/ n.
soul; immaterial, intellectual or mental part of man
精神；灵魂
otherwise /'ʌðəwaiz/ adv.
in another or different way
在其他方面；以另外的方式
erode /i'rəud/ v.
wear away; eat into
腐蚀；侵蚀
subtle /'sʌtl/ adj.
cunning, clever; difficult to perceive
狡猾的，阴险的；难以察觉的
insight /'insait/ n.
understanding; power of seeing into sth with the mind
洞察力，眼光
productivity /ˌprɔdʌk'tiviti/ n.
ability to produce; productive yield
生产（率）
rot /rɔt/ v.
decay or become useless
腐烂；枯朽

father."

6 APPRECIATION

7 Feeling appreciated by others is one of the most basic of human needs. Researchers have found that the quantity of appreciation family members express to one another is even greater than anticipated. One mother wrote, "Each night we go into the children's bedrooms and give each a big **hug** and kiss. Then we say, 'You are really good kids and we love you very much.' We think it's important to leave that message with them at the end of the day."

8 One couple said that appreciation had **literally** changed their life together. "We fell into a **trap** early in our marriage partly because of some couples we saw socially. They considered themselves to be very sophisticated: nothing quite measured up to their standard. One couple delighted in acid sarcasm—especially with each other."

9 "We hadn't realized how their fault-finding and belittling were rubbing off on us. We had begun to see things in a negative way."

10 "We decided to stop. First, we found new friends. Then we began to **accent** the positive. Now when my husband comes home he says, 'I see you've been busy with the boys today and you got your hair cut and did the marketing.' He doesn't **mention** the **weedy** garden."

11 "And when he comes in disappointed over a sale he missed, I remind him of the three he made last week. We've conditioned ourselves to look at what we have, rather than what we lack."

12 COPING WITH CRISIS

13 Strong families are not without problems. But they have the ability to surmount life's **inevitable** challenges when they arise. One of the tools these

---

hug /hʌg/ n.
the act of putting the arms round tightly, esp. to show love
拥抱

literally /'litərəli/ adv.
without exaggeration; strictly, word for word
实在地;完全地

trap /træp/ n.
device for catching animals, etc.; plan for deceiving sb; trick or device to make sb say or do sth he does not wish to do or say
陷阱;诡计

accent /'æksənt/ v.
put emphasis on
强调,使显著

mention /'menʃən/ v.
speak or write sth about; say the name of; refer to
提起;叙述

weedy /'wi:di/ adj.
full of plant where it is not desired
杂草丛生的

inevitable /in'evitəbl/ adj.
unavoidable; certain to happen
不可避免的,一定会发生的

families **identified** as necessary for **coping** with **crisis** is adaptability.

14 At age 40, a Harvard Ph. D. had just about everything he wanted in life. A family man, he had a wife and three children. He was a full professor and a successful writer. Life was moving quickly.

15 It fell apart even more quickly. His wife packed her bags to leave him one Monday. His brother, a heavy smoker, had developed **throat** cancer and his larynx was removed the following Friday. "I looked at his life, and I cried," the professor said. "And then I looked at my own life and I cried."

16 He began to change. He set aside time for his family—time to chat with his young sons while they **snacked**; time to hold the baby. Soon his wife agreed to visit a family therapist with him. She saw that he was exploring a new way to live.

17 The professor had learned what all strong families know. A healthy family is a place we enter for **comfort,** development and **regeneration**; a place from which we go forth **renewed** and charged with power for positive living. As one woman said: "I put love into my family as an **investment** in their future, my future, our future. It's the best investment I can make."

(652 words)

---

identify /aiˈdentifai/ v.
say, show, prove who or what sb or sth is
使等同于；验明

cope /kəup/ v.
(with "with") to deal with a situation, problem
(同 with 连用)对付，处理，解决

crisis (pl. **crises**) /ˈkraisis/ n.
turning point in illness, life, history; time of difficulty
转机；危机

throat /ˈθrəut/ n.
the front part of the neck, the upper part of the passage leading from mouth to the stomach and lungs
喉

snack /snæk/ v.
have a very slight, hurried meal
吃快餐

comfort /ˈkʌmfət/ n.
consolation (for loss, etc.); sb or sth that brings consolation
安慰，抚慰

regeneration /riˌdʒenəˈreiʃən/ n.
being given new life or vigor to
新生；再生

renew /riˈnjuː/ v.
make new again or as if new; revive, reawaken
恢复；更新；变新

investment /inˈvestmənt/ n.
the act of investing, esp. of money
投资

Useful Phrases

(be) known as	regard sb /sth as (being) sth	(被)称之为……
leave sb with sth	give sth to sb; let sb know	给某人留下……
fall into (a trap)	be trapped by sth	落入(陷阱、圈套)
measure up to	reach the standard required or expected	达到……(标准)
(be) delighted in sth/ doing sth	take great pleasure in sth; enjoy sth	乐于……
rub off (cause sth to)	be removed from (a surface) by rubbing	擦掉；磨去
remind sb of sth	cause sb to remember sb/sth	提醒某人注意……
cope with	manage successfully; be able to deal with sth difficult	应付，处理
set aside (time/ money) for...	save or keep (money or time) for a particular purpose	留出，腾出，预留出 (时间、金钱)
go forth	go forward	向前，前进

Proper Nouns

Harvard Ph. D.	哈佛大学博士
the Family Strengths Research Project	幸福家庭研究工程

1. ... an investment otherwise known as commitment... 这种投资又叫义务 (be) known as ……是一个常用句式，意为"被称为……；" known as 可用于系表结构中，也可以放在一名词后作补充说明。

otherwise 意为 in another or different way "在其他方面；以另外的方式"。

be aware of "知道的，明白的，意识到的"。例如：I was not aware of the fire. 我没意识到火。

2. ... nothing quite measured up to their standard. 没有什么事情符合他们的标准。

measure up to "达到（要求、规格、标准）"。

3. ... their fault-finding and belittling were rubbing off on us. 这些人的吹毛求疵、互相贬损在不知不觉地侵蚀着我们。

rub off 意为"擦掉，磨去"。根据上下文，此处的 rub off on sb 应该理解为"……对某人产生负面影响，致使某人原有的优良品质慢慢丢失、减少"。

4. ... when he comes in disappointed over a sale he missed. 他回到家时显得垂头丧气，因为他错过了一笔意。

此处的 disappointed 为动词的过去分词，在句中作伴随方式状语。
此处的 over 有 because of（因为，由于）的意思。

5. One of the tools these families identified as necessary for coping with crisis is adaptability.
解决家庭矛盾的有效方法之一就是不断调整自我，做出某些改变。
identify... as necessary "把……看成是必要的"。

6. It felt apart even more quickly. 这一切顷刻之间就崩溃了。
fall apart "崩溃；坍塌；倒下"。

 **Exercises**

Reading Aloud and Memorizing the Following

I. Read the following paragraph taken from the text until you learn it by heart.

Some families have seen commitment eroded by a more subtle enemy—work, and its demand on time, attention and energy. One father offered this insight: "Sometimes I feel that the time I spend with my sons could be better spent at the office. Then I remind myself that the productivity report will affect life for a few days or weeks. I must do it and it's important, but my job as a father is more important."

The professor had learned what all strong families know. A healthy family is a place we enter for comfort, development and regeneration; a place from which we go forth renewed and charged with power for positive living. As one woman said: "I put love into my family as an investment in their future, my future, our future. It's the best investment I can make."

Comprehension of the Text

II. Choose the best answer to each of the following questions according to the passage.

1. This article is most probably a _____.
   A. university lecture
   B. magazine article
   C. biographical article
   D. humorous short essay

2. According to the author, the following can be considered as qualities for making strong families EXCEPT _____.
   A. an investment of time, energy, spirit and heart
   B. appreciation that family members express
   C. the ability to surmount life's challenges
   D. the wife's loyalty to her husband

3. Which of the following is NOT true as far as commitment is concerned?

   A. Commitment is crucial to a family's success.

   B. Commitment is a kind of investment.

   C. Commitment is often eroded by work.

   D. An extramarital affair (婚外恋) will tend to happen if one values commitment.

4. For a strong family, which of the following is the LEAST important?

   A. Playing together.

   B. Buying toys and owning a comfortable house.

   C. Working together.

   D. Spending time together sufficiently.

5. From the last part of the article, we can know that _____.

   A. the Harvard Ph. D. had a perfect family

   B. the Ph. D.'s happy family was ruined by his ill brother

   C. the Ph. D.'s wife came back and decided to put love into their family as an investment

   D. the Ph. D.'s wife decided to come back because she saw his change and the hope of a new life

III. Answer the following questions with the information you've got from the text.

1. What factors will affect family commitment?   (Para. 3)
2. Why did the parents give their children a big hug and kiss each night?   (Para. 7)
3. Are fault-finding and belittling good or not? Why?   (Para. 9)
4. Why did the wife remind her husband the three sales he made the previous week?   (Para. 11)
5. Why did the Ph. D.'s wife decide to come back?   (Para. 6)

Vocabulary

IV. Spell out the words with the help of the given definitions and the first letters.

1. something needed or required (d_____)

2. do some study in order to discover new fact (r _____)

3. put forward for acceptance, give (o _____)

4. understanding of the nature and quality of something (a _____)

5. something that makes a person, thing imperfect (f _____)

6. make known, show by words, look, actions (e _____)

7. think about (c _____)

8. invitation or call to play a game, run a race, have a fight, etc., to see who is better, stronger (c _____)

9. fail to hit, reach, meet or make contact with (m _____)

10. examine thoroughly problems, etc., in order to test, learn about them (e _____)

V. **Fill in the blanks with the words given below. Change the form where necessary.**

| comfort | quantity | inevitable | identify | mention |
| spirit | anticipate | productivity | crisis | investment |

1. Mr. Brown _____ a large amount of money in the business and has made great profits.

2. Put a little more _____ into your work, and I believe you can do it better.

3. The management is looking for ways of improving _____.

4. In _____ of bad weather they took plenty of warm clothes.

5. We cannot _____ happiness with wealth.

6. Can the price be lower if I buy things in _____ here?

7. They may not be millionaires but they are living a _____ life.

8. In time of _____ it's really good to have a friend to turn to.

9. The train was _____ delayed because of the accident.

10. "Thank you very much for helping me!" "Don't _____ it."

VI. **Fill in the blanks with proper prepositions or adverbs.**

1. May I exchange seat _____ you?

2. We can't hear you. Please speak _____.

3. The young man stole some important papers from the office but later we found him _____.

4. People cannot live _____ air.

5. I must remind you that when you leave here, don't leave anything _____.
6. The pudding was not made _____ my taste. It was too heavy.
7. He and his wife are leaving _____ U. S. tomorrow morning.
8. Man differs most _____ all the other animals in his ability to learn and use language.
9. We shall learn to make the most _____ a bad situation.
10. The police have not looked _____ the case yet.

Structure

VII. Rewrite the following sentences after the models.

> **Model 1** When he comes in disappointed over a sale he missed, **I inform him** of the three he made last week.
>
> > (1) When he comes in disappointed over a sale he missed, **I remind him** of the three he made last week.
> > (2) When he comes in disappointed over a sale he missed, **I remind him** to think about the three he made last week.
> > (3) When he comes in disappointed over a sale he missed, **I remind him** that he made three last week.

1. Do I have to inform you of the fact again?
2. Yesterday he forgot to e-mail his father and I told him to do it.
3. That old photo brought me back to my childhood.
4. The sight of the clock indicated that I was late for school.
5. His mother called him and he remembered to clean his bedroom.

> **Model 2** **Dealing with crisis:** Strong families are not without problems.
> > **Coping with crisis:** Strong families are not without problems.

1. I don't know what to do in front of such an unexpected problem.
2. Tom did very well in solving the conflicts in our company.
3. The CEO managed the crisis successfully with a strong mind.
4. Many people are at a loss in face of a failure.
5. Measures taken made the inflation get worse.

VIII. Study the models and translate the following sentences into English, by using the phrase "set aside" or "fall apart."

Model 1   He **set aside** time for his family.

Model 2   They tried everything to improve their life, but their marriage **fell apart** at last.

1. 他决定今后拿出一部分时间来读书。
2. 政府为这个项目设立了10万元的基金。
3. 她每个星期都要存一点钱。
4. 抽点时间去看看他吧。
5. 他们专门花了很多时间准备新年聚会。
6. 这把旧椅子被他压坍了。
7. 这个计划由于缺乏资金而泡汤了。
8. 这辆汽车撞倒在地而散架了。
9. 项目失败了,他们小组解散了。
10. 当了好多年战俘后他垮了。

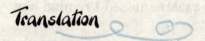

IX. Translate the following sentences into Chinese.

1. Some families have seen commitment eroded by a more subtle enemy.

2. Researchers have found that the quantity of appreciation family members express to one another is even greater than anticipated.

3. Feeling appreciated by others is one of the most basic of human needs.

4. We hadn't realized how their fault-finding and belittling were rubbing off on us.

5. We've conditioned ourselves to look at what we have, rather than what we lack.

X. Translate the following sentences into English using the words or phrases in the brackets.

1. 这把旧椅子在他的重压下快散架了。(fall apart)

2. 我相当赞同你刚才讲的那些话。(appreciate)

3. 年轻人对生活应抱乐观的态度。(positive)

4. 那个村子被称为这个国家最贫穷的地区。(known as)

5. 你预料到会有麻烦吗？(anticipate)

Part II　Grammar

Passive Voice(被动语态)(二)

1. **短语动词被动语态的结构与用法：**

    1) 在英语中，常见的动词短语有三类。以下三类短语动词转换为被动语态时，必须看作是一个动词，其后的介词或副词不能拆开或省略。

    a. "动词＋介词"，如 look after, talk about, deal with 等：

    The baby is well looked after.

    The topic was talked about at the meeting.

    b. "动词＋副词"，如 put off, set up, bring about 等：

    The sports meet has been put off till next week.

    When was the school set up?

    c. "动词＋副词＋介词"，如 face up to, put up with, look down upon 等：

    These difficulties have to be faced up to.

    Such kind of things cannot be put up with.

    2) 除以上三类动词短语之外，还有一种由"动词＋名词＋介词"构成，如 take care of, pay attention to, make fun of 等。转换为被动语态时通常有两种方法：

    一种是把整个短语动词当作一个及物动词处理，如：

    He　took good care of　his baby.　（主动语态）
    主　　　谓　　　　　宾

    His baby　was taken good care of　(by him).　（被动语态）
    　主　　　　　　　谓

    另一种方法是把动词短语看作"动词＋宾语＋介词"结构处理，如：

    He　took good care of　his baby.　　　（主动语态）
    主　　　谓　　　　　宾

    Good care　was taken of　his baby　(by him).　（被动语态）
    　主　　　　　谓　　　　宾

3) 此外，值得注意的是带直接宾语和间接宾语的动词在转换为被动语态时原则上也有两种方法：

一种方法是把间接宾语转变为相应的被动句中的主语，如：

I will give   all my friends   presents   for their birthdays. （主动语态）
主   谓   间接宾语   直接宾语

All my friends   will be given   presents   for their birthdays. （被动语态）
　　主　　　　　　　谓　　　　　　宾　　（被动语态，to 可省略）

另一种是把直接宾语转变为相应被动句的主语，如：

Presents   will be given   to   all my friends   for their birthdays.
　主　　　　　谓　　　　　　　　宾

注：多数情况下把间接宾语（人）作被动句子主语比较自然。

2. 情态动词被动语态的结构与用法：

带情态动词的被动语态由"情态动词＋be＋动词过去分词"构成，这种被动可以是一般形式，也可以是完成体形式。如：

The work cannot be finished before Friday.

The boy might be raised in a single parent family.

The rules must be paid attention to.

Her hair must have been dyed. (表示对过去发生的事情的推测)

He should not have been told the fact. (表示过去不该做但做了的事情)

Exercises

I. Change the following sentences into the passive voice, using two forms when possible.

1. The Greens talked over important things together.
2. A piano takes up most of the space in the small room.
3. The film took everybody in.
4. We could not put up with the noise any more.
5. We hardly ever made use of this possibility.
6. Mary realized that they were making fun of her.

7. They never paid attention to the matter.
8. We must put an end to the situation as soon as possible.
9. Everyone looked up to him.
10. You must lay special emphasis on the choice of words.
11. We could hardly see each other in the fog.
12. People mustn't leave bicycles in the hall.
13. You needn't type this letter now.
14. You should have taken those books back to the library.
15. You can find answers to the exercises in the teacher's book.

II. Translate the following sentences into English, using the passive voice.

1. 这本书里提到了几种学习方法。

2. 这个坏习惯应该改掉。

3. 这条路必须在年底之前修好。

4. 我们应该多花些时间与家人在一起。

5. 爱可以作为投资放到家里。

Part III Reading Practice

Guide to Reading

1. **Words and Expressions to Learn**

self-esteem	n.	自尊
belief	n.	信仰;信奉
communicate	v.	交流;通知;联络
interact	v.	相互作用;相互影响
manageable	adj.	易管理的;易处理的;易操纵的
individual	adj.&n.	个人(的),个体(的);个别(的),单独的
ultimately	adv.	最后,最终;终于
treatment	n.	对待;待遇;治疗;处置
behavior	n.	行为,举止
reality	n.	现实;真实;实物
handle	v.	处理,应付;操作
threaten	v.	威胁
rude	adj.	粗暴的,不礼貌的
rough	adj.	艰苦的;崎岖的
normal	adj.	正常的
external	adj.	外部的;外在的;客观的
exchange	v./n.	交换
rely	v.	依赖,依靠
comment	v.&n.	评论,评语;意见

2. **Pre-Reading Questions**

   (1) What do we need to form the basis of a child's self-esteem?

   (2) How will a child feel if he or she grows up without feeling of self-esteem?

The Function and Creation of Self-esteem

1   Self-esteem is what people think about themselves—whether or not they feel valued—and when family members have self-respect, pride, and belief in themselves, this high self-esteem makes it possible to cope with the everyday problems of growing up.

2   Successful parenting begins by communicating to children that they belong, and are loved for not other reason than just because they exist. Through touch and tone of voice parents tell their **infants** (*n.* 婴儿) whether or not they are valued, special and loved, and it is these messages that form the basis of the children's self-esteem. When children grow up with love and are made to feel lovable despite their mistakes and failures, they are able to interact with others in a responsible, honest, and loving way. A healthy self-esteem is a **resource** (*n.* 应付办法) for coping when difficulties arise, making it easier to see a problem as **temporary** (*adj.* 暂时的), manageable, and something from which the individual can emerge.

3   If, however, children grow up without love and without feeling of self-esteem, they feel unlovable and worthless and expect to be cheated, **taken advantage of** (被利用), and looked down upon by others. Ultimately their actions invite this treatment, and their self-defeating behavior turns expectations into reality. They do not have the personal resources to handle everyday problems in a healthy way, and life may be viewed as just one crisis after another. Without a healthy self-esteem they may cope by acting out problems rather than talking them out or by **withdrawing** (*v.* 退缩) and remaining **indifferent** (*adj.* 漠不关心的) toward themselves and others. These individuals grow up to live **isolated** (*adj.* 孤独的), lonely lives, lacking the ability to give the love that they have never received.

4   Self-esteem is a kind of energy, and when it is high, people feel like they can handle anything. It is what one feels when special things are happening or everything is going great. A word of praise, a smile, a good grade on a report card, or doing something that creates pride within oneself can create this energy. When feelings about the self have been threatened and self-esteem is low, everything

becomes more of an effort. It is difficult to hear, see, or think clearly, and others seem rude, **inconsiderate** (*adj.* 不替他人考虑的), and rough. The problem is not with others, it is with the self, but often it is not until energies are back to normal that the real problem is recognized.

5   The infant's self-esteem is totally dependent on family members, and it is not until about the time the child enters school that outside forces **contribute to** (促成) feelings about the self. A child must also learn that a major resource for a healthy self-esteem comes from within. Some parents raise their children to depend on external rather than internal **reinforcement** (*n.* 强化) through practices such as paying for good grades or report cards or exchanging special **privileges** (*n.* 特权) for good behavior. The child learns to rely on others to maintain a high self-esteem and is not prepared to live in a world in which desirable behavior does not automatically produce a **tangible** (*adj.* 实实在在的) reward such as a smile, money, or special privileges.

6   Maintaining a healthy self-esteem is a challenge that continues throughout life. One family found that they could help each other identify positive attitudes. One evening during an electric storm the family gathered around the kitchen table and each person wrote down two things that they liked about each family member. These pieces of paper were folded and given to the **appropriate** (*adj.* 合适的) person, who one by one opened their special messages. The father later commented, "It was quite an experience, opening each little piece of paper and reading the message. I still have those gifts, and when I've had a really bad day, I read through them and I always come away feeling better."

7   The foundation of a healthy family depends on the ability of the parents to communicate messages of love, trust and self worth to each child. This is the basis on which self-esteem is built, and as the child grows, self-esteem changes from a collection of others' feeling to become personal feelings about the self. Ultimately a person's self-esteem is reflected in the way he or she interacts with others.

(*696 words*)

Reading Comprehension

I. Answer the following questions according to the passage.

1. What is self-esteem?
2. What forms the basis of children's self-esteem?
3. What are the possible results for the children without self-esteem?
4. What helps create the energy of self-esteem?
5. What can parents do to found a healthy family?

II. Translate into Chinese the following sentences taken from the passage.

1. When family members have self-respect, pride, and belief in themselves, this high self-esteem makes it possible to cope with the everyday problems of growing up.
2. They do not have the personal resources to handle everyday problems in a healthy way.
3. Self-esteem is a kind of energy, and when it is high, people feel like they can handle anything.
4. If children grow up without love and without feeling of self-esteem, they feel unlovable and worthless.
5. It is not until about the time the child enters school that outside forces contribute to feelings about the self.

III. Fill in the blanks with the words or phrases listed in Words and Expressions to Learn. Change the form where necessary.

1. She _____ towards me more like a friend than a mother.
2. _____ it or not, we were waiting in the rain for two hours.
3. Being deaf and dump makes _____ very difficult.
4. That's an excuse. Please tell me the _____ reason.
5. Ann _____ seats with Ben because she could not see the blackboard clearly in the back row.

6. Weeping is a _____ response to pain.
7. I've never been treated so _____.
8. He played an important role this time by making great _____ to the project.
9. The worsening environment is a great _____ to human beings.
10. Compared with the rights of the society, that of the _____ is of less importance.

Part IV Practical English

Business Correspondences(业务信函)(二)

4. Letters of Thanks

感谢信是受到对方某种恩惠,如受到邀请、接待、慰问,收到礼品以及得到帮助等之后,向对方表达感谢之情的信函。

通用格式:

1. 日期。
2. 称谓。
3. 说明为什么要感谢。
4. 再次表示致谢、问候。
5. 署名。

Sample

Dec. 27, 2006

Dear Sandy:

　　When you left a package for me yesterday, I had difficulty waiting until my birthday to open it.

　　I don't know how to thank you for such an attractive present. It is something that will give me pleasure for a long time to come.

　　Please accept my sincere thanks and best wishes.

Cordially,
(Signature)
Susan

亲爱的桑迪：

你昨天给我留下一个包裹，我真是很难等到生日那天才打开！

我真不知该怎样感谢你送给我这么漂亮的礼物。它会给我带来莫大的快乐的。

请接受我诚挚的感激和最好的祝福。

诚挚的

（签名）

苏珊

2006年12月27日

Useful Expressions

1. Thank you very much for...
   十分感谢……

2. Many thanks for your...
   非常感谢您……

3. Please accept my sincere appreciation for...
   请接受我对……真挚的感谢。

4. I am truly grateful to you for...
   为了……，我真心感激您。

5. It was good (thoughtful) of you...
   承蒙好意（关心）……

6. You were so kind to send...
   承蒙好意送来……

7. Thank you again for your wonderful hospitality and I am looking forward to seeing you soon.
   再次感谢您的盛情款待，并期待不久见到您。

8. I find an ordinary "thank-you" entirely inadequate to tell you how much...
   我觉得一般的感谢的字眼完全不足以表达我对您是多么的……

9. I sincerely appreciate...
   我衷心地感谢……

10. I wish to express my profound appreciation for...
    我对……深表谢意。

5. Letters of Congratulations

祝贺信是向对方表示祝贺的信件,凡是遇到重大的喜庆节日,如圣诞节、新年、婚礼和生日等等,亲友间要写祝贺信。当亲友晋升、毕业、考试成功或出国留学时也要写祝贺信。祝贺信相对而言是比较容易写的,但用词必须亲切有礼,表达出真诚的喜悦感情。

Sample

May 16, 2006

Dear Ruth,

  I offer my warmest congratulations on your promotion to Vice President of the company. I know how talented you are and how hard you've worked to attain this goal. No one could have been more deserving. How exciting it must be for you to realize your ambitions after all those years of hard working. It's been a real encouragement to me to see your efforts rewarded.

  Sincere congratulations to you. Your expertise and dedication will bring out the best of everyone on your staff. They're learning from a real professional.

  I wish you still further success.

Sincerely yours,
(Signature)
Ma Lin

亲爱的鲁思：

听说你当选了公司副总裁我表示热烈的祝贺。我知道你很有天赋，而且为了实现这个目标你付出了很大的努力。没人比你更应该得到这个职位。这么多年的努力终于得到了回报，你该多么高兴啊。你的成功对我来说是个莫大的鼓励。

真诚地祝贺你。你的专业和奉献将使公司所有员工都能发挥自己的最佳水平。他们是在学习一个真正的专业人士。

预祝你取得更大的成功。

你的朋友：
（签名）
马林
2006年5月16日

Useful Expressions

1. Congratulations, all of us feel proud of your remarkable achievements!
   祝贺你，我们都为你所取得的巨大成就感到骄傲。

2. I am so pleased and happy to hear that...
   听到……我真的非常高兴。

3. I write to congratulate you upon...
   我写信来祝贺你……

4. I offer you my warmest congratulations on your...
   对于你的……我表示热烈的祝贺。

5. We are just as proud as can be of you and send our congratulations.
   我们为你感到由衷的自豪！祝贺你！

6. I wish you still further success!
   预祝你取得更大的成功。

7. We look forward to bragging about you in the years ahead.
   我们希望在未来的岁月中能骄傲地谈起你。

8. Please accept our most sincere congratulations and very best wishes for all the good future in the world.
   谨向你表示祝贺和最良好的祝福。

Writing Practice

I. The following sentences go together to form a letter of thanks, but they are in the wrong order. Put them right.

> 15 August, 2006
>
> Dear Marian,
>
>   I had not told anybody about it.
>
>   Imagine my happiness at seeing your lovely present!
>
>   Just what I need as we are all training hard for the coming tennis tournament.
>
>   How did you find out that it was my birthday yesterday?
>
>   A pair of sun-glasses for sports use!
>
>   The sun will not hurt my eyes any more!
>
>   My gratitude!
>
>   Yours,
>
>   (Signature)
>
>   Nan

II. Complete the following letter according to the Chinese versions.

> 尊敬的部长先生：
>
>   请允许我向您升任贸易部长表示祝贺。多年来您对国家的贡献被认可、欣赏，我非常高兴。我们祝愿您在新的职位取得成功，期待我们两国在贸易发展上进一步合作。
>
>   诚挚的
>
>   （签名）
>
>   约翰·理查德
>
>   2006 年 8 月 15 日

15 August, 2006

Dear Mr. Minister,

　　Allow me to convey my congratulations _____ (1) your promotion to Minister of Trade. I am delighted _____ (2) many years' service you have given to your country should have been _____ (3) and appreciated.

　　We wish you _____ (4) in your new post and look forward to closer cooperation with you in the development of trade _____ (5) our two countries.

Sincerely,
(Signature)
John Richard

Part V English Salon

1. Wisdom in the mind is better than money in the hand.
2. Nothing is impossible for a willing heart.
3. All things are difficult before they are easy.
4. Great hopes make great man.
5. God helps those who help themselves.

Try to find the Chinese equivalent for the above proverbs.

Unit Six

Part I TEXT

Guide to Text-Learning

1. **Words and Expressions Related to the Topic**

organ	(人体)器官
tissue	(人体)组织
cell	(人体)细胞
neuron	神经细胞
neurotransmitter	神经传递素
nerve	神经
gland	腺
muscle	肌肉
synapse	(神经元的)触处;突触
skull	头盖骨,头颅
receptor	神经末梢
glucose	葡萄糖
vitamin	维生素
mineral	矿物质
virus	病毒

2. **Grammatical Structures to Learn**

   (1) Electrical signals **either** reach parts of the machine **or** they do not.
   电子信号传递或是不传递到机内某些部件上。

   (2) In the nervous system, neurons are **more than** just on or off.
   在神经系统中,神经细胞的工作方式远远不是"开"或"关"那么简单了。

(3) The external and internal components of computers and brains **are all susceptible to** damage.
计算机和人脑的内外部件都容易受到损伤。

(4) Your computer should be **as good as new**.
你的计算机又会像新的一样能正常工作。

Warming-Up Questions:

1. What is the function of the human brain?
2. What are the similarities between the human brain and a computer?
3. What are the differences between the human brain and a computer?

A Computer in Your Head

1   What has billions of **individual** pieces, **trillions** of **connections,** weighs about 1.4 kilograms, and works on electrochemical energy? If you guessed a minicomputer, you're wrong. If you guessed the human brain, you're correct! The human brain: a **mass** of white-pink tissue that allows you to ride a bike, read a book, laugh at a joke, and remember your friend's phone number. And that's just for starters. Your brain controls your emotions, **appetite**, sleep, heart rate, and breathing. Your brain is who you are and everything you will be.

2   The amazing brain has been **compared** to many different objects and devices—from a **spider** web to a clock to

individual /ˌindiˈvidjuəl/ *adj.*	
single; separate	
个别的；单个的，个人的	
trillion /ˈtriljən/ *n.&pron.*	
one million million million	
一兆，一万亿	
connection /kəˈnekʃən/ *n.*	
being connected	
连接	
mass /ˈmæs/ *n.*	
a large solid lump or pile	
团；块	
appetite /ˈæpitait/ *n.*	
desire, esp. for food	
胃口；食欲	
compare /kəmˈpeə/ *v.*	
examine people or things to see how they are alike and how they are different	
比较	
spider /ˈspaidə/ *n.*	
any of many kinds of small creatures which make silk threads into nets for catching insects to eat	
蜘蛛	

a telephone **switchboard**. Nowadays, people like to compare it to a computer. Is your brain really like the **metal** box that **hums** on your desk? Let's look at the **similarities** and differences between the two.

3   Computers and brains both need energy. **Plug** your computer into the wall, push a **button**, and it will get the power it needs to run. Pull the plug and it will shut down. Your brain operates in a different way. It gets its energy in the form of glucose from the food you eat. Your **diet** also provides essential materials, such as vitamins and minerals, for **proper** brain function. **Unlike** a computer, your brain has no OFF **switch**. Even when you are asleep, your brain is active. Although computers and brains are powered by different types of energy, they both use electrical **signals** to transmit information. Computers send electrical signals through wires to control devices. Your brain also sends electrical signals, but it sends them through nerve cells, called neurons. Signals in neurons **transfer** information to other neurons and control glands, organs, or muscles.

4   There are fundamental differences in the way information is transferred through electrical **circuits** in a computer and through nerve cells in your brain. When a computer is turned on, electrical signals either reach parts of the machine or they do not. In other

---

switchboard /ˈswɪtʃˌbɔːd/ *n.*
place where telephone lines in a large building are connected
电话总机

metal /ˈmetl/ *n.*
a hard, usually shiny substance used to make machines, etc.
金属的

hum /hʌm/ *v.*
buzz; sing with closed lips
发嗡嗡声

similarity /ˌsɪmɪˈlærɪti/ *n.*
being similar; likeness; similar feature or aspect
相似(性)

plug /plʌɡ/ *v.*
insert sth into
接上插头通电

button /ˈbʌtn/ *n.*
a switch on a machine
按钮

diet /ˈdaɪət/ *n.*
food and drink usually taken
饮食；食物

proper /ˈprɔpə/ *adj.*
right; suitable
合适的；恰当的

unlike /ʌnˈlaɪk/ *adj. & prep.*
not like; different from
不像(的)；与……不同(的)

switch /swɪtʃ/ *n.*
apparatus for stopping or starting an electronic current
开关；电闸

signal /ˈsɪɡnl/ *n.*
a sound or action to warn, command or give message
信号

transfer /trænsˈfəː/ *v.*
move sth or sb from one place to another; change; move
传递

circuit /ˈsəːkɪt/ *n.*
circular path of an electric current
电路

words, the computer uses switches that are either on or off. In the nervous system, neurons are more than just on or off. An individual neuron may receive information from thousands of other neurons. The region where information is transferred from one neuron to another is called the synapse. A small **gap** between neurons is located at the synapse. When information is transferred from one neuron to another, **molecules** of chemicals are **released** from the end of one neuron. The neurotransmitters travel across the gap to reach a receiving neuron, where they **attach** to **special** structures called receptors. This results in a small electrical response **within** the receiving neuron. However, this small response does not mean that the message will continue. Remember, the receiving neuron may be getting thousands of small signals at many synapses. Only when the **total** signal from all of these synapses **exceeds** a certain **level** will a large signal be **generated** and the message continue.

5   The **delicate** contents inside your computer are protected by a hard cover. Your skull provides a similar function for your brain. The **external** and **internal components** of computers and brains are all **susceptible** to damage. If you

---

gap /'gæp/ *n.*
opening or break in sth
间隙；缺口，裂口

molecule /'mɔlikjuːl/ *n.*
the smallest unit into which any substance can be divided without losing its own chemical nature
（化学）分子

release /ri'liːs/ *v.*
set free
释放

attach /ə'tætʃ/ *v.*
fasten; cause to join
依附

special /'speʃəl/ *adj.*
not ordinary or usual; of a particular kind
特别的；专门的

within /wi'ðin/ *prep.*
inside; not more than
在……之内

total /'təutl/ *adj.*
complete; whole
总的；总共的

exceed /ik'siːd/ *v.*
be greater than; do more than
超过

level /'levəl/ *n.*
a degree of attainment
水平；(一定) 的标准

generate /'dʒenə,reit/ *v.*
produce; cause sth to occur
生成；产生

delicate /'delikit/ *adj.*
tender; fine; easily broken or injured
精致的；易破的

external /eks'tɜːnl/ *adj.*
on, of, or for the outside
外部的；外面的

internal /in'tɜːnl/ *adj.*
of or on the inside
内部的；里面的

component /kəm'pəunənt/ *n.*
any of the parts of which sth is made
组件，部件

susceptible /sə'septəbl/ *adj.*
likely to suffer from
敏感的；易受影响或损害的

drop your computer, **infect** it with a virus, or leave it on during a huge power **surge**, your precious machine will **likely** be on its way to the repair shop. When damaged parts are replaced or the virus-caused damage is removed, your computer should be as good as new. Unfortunately, brains are not as easy to repair. They are **fragile** and there are no replacement parts to fix damaged brain tissue. However, hope is on the **horizon** for people with brain damage and **neurological** disorders, as scientists **investigate** ways to **transplant** nerve cells and repair injured brains.

No doubt the biggest difference between a computer and your brain is **consciousness**. Although it may be difficult for you to describe consciousness, you know you are here. Computers do not have such awareness. Although computers can perform **extraordinary computational feats** at **astounding** speeds, they do not **experience** the emotions, dreams, and thoughts that are an essential part of what makes us human. At least not yet! Current research in **artificial** intelligence is moving toward developing emotional **capabilities** in computers and **robots**.

(710 words)

---

infect /inˈfekt/ v.
cause sb or sth to have a disease
传染，使受感染

surge /sɜːdʒ/ n.
a sudden abnormal rise of current followed by a drop
汹涌；冲动

likely /ˈlaikli/ adj.&adv.
probable; probably
很可能(的)；大概；多半

fragile /ˈfrædʒail/ adj.
easily broken or damaged
易碎的

horizon /həˈraizn/ n.
line where the sky seems to meet the earth or sea
地平线

neurological /njuərəuˈlɔdʒikəl/ adj.
of scientific study of nerves and their diseases
神经学(上)的

investigate /inˈvestigeit/ v.
inquire carefully about
调查；了解

transplant /trænsˈplɑːnt/ v.
take an organ from one person and put it into another
(器官)移植

consciousness /ˈkɔnʃəsnis/ n.
all the ideas, feelings, opinions held by a person
意识

extraordinary /iksˈtrɔːdnri/ adj.
beyond what is usual
非凡的；惊人的

computational /ˌkɔmpju(ː)ˈteiʃ(ə)n(ə)l/ adj.
of calculation
计算方面的；使用计算机的

feat /fiːt/ n.
difficult action successfully done
伟绩；功绩

astounding /əˈstaundiŋ/ adj.
amazing
令人惊奇的

experience /iksˈpiəriəns/ v.
undergo; feel
经历；体验；具有

artificial /ɑːtiˈfiʃəl/ adj.
made by humans; lacking true
人(工)造的

capability /ˌkeipəˈbiliti/ n.
the quality of being capable
能力

robot /ˈrəubɔt/ n.
a computer controlled machine which can move and do some of the work of a human being
机器人

Useful Phrases

in the form of	in a particular kind of arrangement or structure	以……的方式
in other words	explain sth in another way	换句话说
shut down	turn off	关闭
at least	at the minimum estimate	至少
as good as new	being of the same quality of sth new	同……一样好(新);如同新的一样
no doubt	without any uncertainty	毫无疑问
more than	surpassing; exceeding	超过;不只是
compare sth to sth	examine two things to see how they are like	比作……
compare sth with sth	examine people or things to see how they are alike and how they are different	比较
attach to	fasten or join one thing to another	依附在……上
result in	bring about	导致……的出现;引来……;造成……
be susceptible to	easily affected by	容易遭致……
be on the horizon	likely to come out or happen	有希望;……有可能出现

Notes

1 And that's just for starters.
这还仅仅是(对大脑)最初步的认识。
starter 本意为"初学者,起步者",根据上下文应理解为"对……的初步认识"。

2. There are fundamental differences in the way information is transferred through electrical circuits in a computer and through nerve cells in your brain. 计算机和人脑传输信息的方式有着根本的不同:计算机是通过电路来传输信息,而人脑是通过神经细胞来传输信息。

"in the way..." 后面常用一个句子来修饰限定,意为"在……方面"。

3. In the nervous system, neurons are more than just on or off. 在神经系统里,神经远远不只是"开"和"关"这么简单。

more than 在这里的意思为"超过;不仅仅是",后面可以跟名词。

4. Only when the total signal from all of these synapses exceeds a certain level will a large signal be generated and the message continue. 只有在所有这些突触接收到的信号总量超过一定程度时,一个大的信号才会产生,信号的传递也才能继续。

注意这个句子的语序。当由 only 引导的状语放在句首时,主句应当使用倒装语序 will a large signal be generated...

5. ...your precious machine will likely be on its way to the repair shop. 你那宝贝机器(计算机)就很有可能要送到维修店去修理了。

be on one's way to ..."在去……的路上"。

6. Unfortunately, brains are not as easy to repair. 不幸的是,人脑的修复却不那么容易。

句中的 as 表示了同另一对象(计算机)在修复方面的比较。

7. ... hope is on the horizon for people with brain damage and neurological disorders... 那些脑部受损、神经系统出现紊乱的患者已经看到希望。

be on the horizon 意思为"在地平线上,刚冒出地平线",根据上下文,可理解为"看到希望"。

8. At least not yet! 至少目前还没有。

at least "至少"。这是个有所省略的句子。not yet 可看成是 they have not yet experienced... 的省略。

Reading Aloud and Memorizing the Following

I. Read the following paragraph taken from the text until you learn it by heart.

No doubt the biggest difference between a computer and your brain is consciousness. Although it may be difficult for you to describe consciousness, you know you are here. Computers do not have such awareness. Although computers can perform extraordinary computational feats at astounding speeds, they do not experience the emotions, dreams, and thoughts that are an essential part of what makes us human. At least not yet! Current research in artificial intelligence is moving toward developing emotional capabilities in computers and robots.

Comprehension of the Text

II. Choose the best answer to each of the following questions according to the passage.

1. The massage mainly tells us _____.
   A. how powerful the human brain is
   B. what the future computers will do for man
   C. some similarities and differences between computers and human brains
   D. a damaged computer can be repaired but the human brain cannot

2. People often compare computers to human brains because _____.
   A. computers can do all the things man can do
   B. computers also need energy as man does
   C. computers can perform many extraordinary feats at astounding speed
   D. computers can be made as small as human brains

3. The fundamental difference between a computer and the human brain is _____.
   A. the way information is transferred
   B. the fact that there is no switch in the human brain

C. the fact that there are electric circuits in a computer, but not in the human brain
   D. that a part in a computer can receive only one signal at a time while a cell in the human brain can receive many signals at a time
4. The word neurotransmitters in the passage means _____.
   A. many neurons
   B. electric signals
   C. receptors
   D. molecules of chemicals
5. The author's attitude towards the development of the medical science is _____.
   A. positive
   B. negative
   C. indifferent
   D. doubtful

III. Answer the following questions with the information you've got from the text.

1. What is the human brain like and how does it work? (Para. 1)
2. What similarities do computers and human brains have? (Para. 3, 5)
3. What is the difference between computers and human brains in the way information is transferred? (Para. 4)
4. Can an injured brain be repaired? If not, why? (Para. 5)
5. What will the future computers be like? (Para. 6)

Vocabulary

IV. Spell out the words with the help of the given definitions and the first letters.

1. the organ in the head that controls thought (b _____)
2. single; separate (i _____)
3. supply; arrange for sb to get (p _____)
4. made by human; lacking true (a _____)
5. set free; allow to be known and printed (r _____)

6. the parts of a whole (c _____)
7. a sound or action intended to warn, command, or give a message (s _____)
8. hurt; damage (i _____)
9. move sth/sb from one place to another; change, move (t _____)
10. examine people or things to see how they are alike and how they are different (c _____)

V. Fill in the blanks with the words given below. Change the form where necessary.

| attach | exceed | gap | describe | investigate |
| experience | special | capable | diet | connect |

1. We all agree that _____ is the preparation for giving advice.
2. The computer looks nothing _____ but its computational feats are extraordinary.
3. When we send an e-mail to someone, we often include a (n) _____ which may be a text, or a picture or a video clip.
4. The story gives a vivid _____ of the superwoman.
5. We are told that the case is under _____ .
6. Do you really believe that there is a _____ between the old generation and the young generation?
7. The CEO worries that the cost of the products of this month will _____ that of last month.
8. A person with liver trouble should take low-fat _____ .
9. A powerful country depends much on its workers' _____ for technical innovation.
10. His journey to Japan is in _____ with his doctoral dissertation.

VI. Fill in the blanks with proper prepositions or adverbs.

1. Will you please turn _____ your stereo a little, it's too loud and I can't concentrate on my writing.
2. American Civil War broke _____ on April 12, 1861.
3. Late at night, someone dug a big hole _____ the wall.
4. The Siamese twins (连体双胎新生婴儿) were separated _____ the back of the head, one child survived but the other died soon.

5. A personal description is painting a picture of a person _____ words.
6. Hearing the soft knock, the old man got up from the bed and peered out his door _____ the night.
7. The police found the kidnapped child frozen _____ fear.
8. After a two-hour meeting, I hurried out of the room _____ a breath of open air.
9. The school band enjoys a good reputation _____ students.
10. When they were young, they used to hang out _____ the same corner.

Structure

VII. Rewrite the following sentences after the models.

Model 1   When a computer is turned on, electrical signals sometimes reach parts of the machine. Sometimes they do not.

> When a computer is turned on, electrical signals **either** reach parts of the machine **or** they do not.

1. You can park on either side of the street.
2. You can request a copy by writing or phoning.
3. I left the book on the table, and if not, in the drawer.
4. One of them—Tom, Tony and Tim—will come to my party.
5. Jane said angrily, "If you don't say sorry to me, get out!"

Model 2   Neurons are not just on or off.

> Neurons are **more than** just on or off.

1. It is not just a problem of quality only.
2. I am very very sorry for my being late.
3. Judging from the five-year-old boy's bravery, he was like an adult.
4. When making a decision, profit is not the only one aspect we need to consider.
5. Besides what is listed on the blackboard, you should read more books.

VIII. Study the models and translate the sentences into English by using the phrase "be susceptible to..." or "as good as..."

Model 1   The external and internal components of computers and brains <u>are susceptible to</u> damage.

Model 2   Your computer should be <u>as good as new</u>.

1. 她易受过去的影响。
2. 这个孩子体质弱,很容易感冒。
3. 汤姆太缺乏主见,容易受别人影响。
4. 这台装置很容易受到损坏,你可要当心。
5. 别用力拉那绳子,它容易断。
6. 她的回答实际上等于是拒绝。
7. 我的车虽然用了很长时间,但它还像新的一样。
8. 他模仿的像真的一样。
9. 这张油画看上去像是真的。
10. 他的赞誉听起来就像是反话。

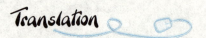

IX. Translate the following sentences into Chinese.

1. It gets its energy in the form of glucose from the food you eat.

2. Unlike a computer, your brain has no OFF switch.

3. The neurotransmitters travel across the gap to reach a receiving neuron, where they attach to special structures called receptors.

4. When information is transferred from one neuron to another, molecules of chemicals are released from the end of one neuron.

5. Although computers can perform extraordinary computational feats at astounding speeds, they do not experience the emotions, dreams, and thoughts that are an essential part of what makes us human. At least not yet!

Part II Grammar

Subordinate Clauses(从句)(一)

从句(一)名词从句 (Noun Clause)

在句子中起名词作用的句子叫名词从句。名词从句的功能相当于名词词组,它在复合句中能担任主语、宾语、表语、同位语、介词宾语等。根据它在句中不同的语法功能,名词从句又可分为主语从句、宾语从句、表语从句和同位语从句。

名词从句应由引导名词性从句的连接词引出。这些连词可分为三类:

1. that 无具体意思,仅起引导一般陈述句的作用,在从句中不担当任何成分,引导宾语从句时有时可省去。
2. whether, if 意为"是否",起引导一般疑问句的作用,在从句中不担当任何成分;从句要用陈述句语序。
3. 连接代词:who, whoever, whom, whomever, which (which…), what, whatever, whose (whose…)

连接副词:when, where, why, how

连接代词和连接副词自身有具体的意思,用来引导含有特殊疑问的句子,连接代词和连接副词要在从句中充当句子成分。从句同样要使用陈述句语序。

1. 宾语从句

1) 用作主句中及物动词的宾语,这类动词通常有:say, think, insist, hope, suppose, believe, agree, expect, explain, order, suggest, demand, feel, know, wonder, ask, realize, understand 等。例如:

We never doubt **(that) he is honest**.

I don't know **if (whether) he is still in the office**, for it is lunch time.

Nobody can tell **when she will arrive.**

The club will give a prize to **whoever wins.**

She asked me **where I was off to.**

We wondered **why Mary left in a hurry**.

I cannot understand **how you can accomplish the task in so short a time.**

2) 用作动词短语的宾语, 如:

Take care **(that) nothing goes wrong with the computer.**

Keep in mind **what the teacher said about the test.**

It depends on **whether you can understand the text.**

You must give it back to **whomever it belongs to.**

We are worrying about **where we shall go**.

2. 主语从句

主语从句在主句中作主语, 例如:

That you don't believe me is a great mistake.

What caused the fire is still a mystery.

Whose suggestion will be adopted is well preserved.

Whether Laura comes or not doesn't concern me.

How the goods will sell depends on the way the boss operates the store.

Why he is so busy recently is not known to any of us.

Who will take over the president of the committee has not been decided yet.

Which would be the best birthday gift for his mother bothered Mr. Green greatly.

When the results of the exam will come out is not yet clear.

3. 表语从句

表语从句在句中作表语。例如:

The question is **why he likes the place so much.**

The fact is **that he didn't notice the car until too late.**

The problem is **what we can do to deal with the situation now.**

The point is **whether we should lend him the money.**

Their current worry is **where they can go after being dismissed.**

That's **what I hope for.**

The topic of today's meeting is **which design will be chosen for our project.**

此外，because 也可引导表语从句，例如：

The reason I haven't been fired is **because my boss is too busy to consider it.**

4. 同位语从句

常常跟在 fact, idea, opinion, news, hope, belief 等名词后面。同位语从句一般用来解释或说明这些名词的具体含义或内容，在逻辑上表现为同位关系。例如：

They are familiar with the opinion **that all matter consists of atoms**.
他们很熟悉这一观点，所有的物质都是由原子构成的。

They were delighted at the news **that their team had won**.
当听到他们的球队赢了的消息时，他们欣喜若狂。

The news **that he will leave for Shanghai** is true.
他将要去上海的消息是真的。

5. 形式主语与形式宾语

1) 当主语为从句时，可以用 it 作形式主语，把主语从句后置。结构通常为：

形式主语 it ＋谓语部分＋主语从句

　It is possible **that Mary will come later.**

　It was a surprise **that Tom did very well in the final exam.**

注：用 it 作形式主语的 "that- 从句" 有以下四种不同的搭配关系：

a. It ＋ be ＋形容词＋ that- 从句

　It is necessary / important / obvious that...

b. It ＋ be ＋ -ed 分词＋ that- 从句

　It is believed / known / has been decided that...

c. It ＋ be ＋名词＋ that- 从句

　It is common knowledge / a surprise / a fact that...

d. It ＋不及物动词＋ that- 分句

　It appears / happens / occurred to me that...

2) 宾语从句用作复合宾语的一部分，其后还有宾语补足语时，这时需用 it 作形式宾语，而把宾语从句放在宾语补足语的后面。如：

I remember (that) I made **it** clear to you **that the paper should be handed in within this week.**

We all think **it** a pity **that you cannot come to the party.**

Exercises

I. Translate the following sentences into English with subordinate clauses.

1. 没人知道她来还是不来。
2. 谁为这起车祸负责还不太清楚。
3. 请你解释一下这个为什么错了。
4. 想吃什么就吃吧。
5. 问题不是谁要走而是谁要留下。
6. 我想知道他的学习是如何进步得如此快的。
7. 吉姆不得不面对考试不及格的事实。
8. 你昨天所说的话大大地伤害了她的感情。
9. 我不在乎你是否喜欢该计划。
10. 我想他不会喜欢你的礼物。

II. Rewrite the following sentences with the formal subject "it."

1. What you say does not matter in the least.
2. That you should feel responsible for our failure is totally wrong.
3. He clearly indicated that he didn't want to speak to me.
4. People don't know whether there was gold left in the mine.
5. He believed that he could deliver a speech on behalf of the school was an honor.

III. Correct the following sentences.

1. I don't know where are you going.
2. It was decided that the meeting will be put off till the next Monday.
3. He suggests that she does the work alone.
4. It is not known that when we shall have a holiday.
5. The mystery is if he ever went there at all.

Part III Reading Practice

Guide to Reading

1. Words and Expressions to Learn

contact	n.	接触,联系
destroy	v.	破坏;消灭
host	n.	主人,东道主
monitor	v.	监测;监视
replace	v.	取代,替换
risk	n.	风险,危险
battery	n.	电池
induce	v.	引起;诱导
leak	v.	漏;渗透
permanent	adj.	永久的;长期不变的
virus	n.	病毒
bacteria	n.	(bacterium 的复数)细菌
bulb	n.	电灯泡
donor	n.	捐献者
fluid	n.&adj.	液体;不稳定的
immune	adj.	免疫的;不受影响的
invade	v.	侵略;侵占
meanwhile	adv.	当时;同时
temporarily	adv.	暂时地;临时地
transplant	v.	移植
whilst	conj.	(=while)当……的时候

145

2. Pre-Reading Questions

(1) How important are the organs in the body?
(2) What is the vital danger after the transplantation?

Organ Transplantation

1   If a battery runs out in a toy, it is easily replaced. When a light bulb stops working, it takes just a few moments to remove the old bulb and put in a new one. When organs of the body fail for whatever reason, replacing them is not nearly so simple!

2   When a potential donor organ becomes available, there is a great deal to do. The tissue type of the donor must be matched as closely as possible with a person needing an organ transplant. There are two operating teams working at the same time, sometimes in the same hospital, sometimes in other parts of the country or even in another country. One team removes the organs from the body of the organ donor and packs them in specially prepared boxes for a transplanting to the operating theatre, where they are needed for a transplant. Meanwhile, the other team will be preparing the **recipient** (*n.* 接受者) to receive his new organ.

3   It is important that the donor organ is ready and waiting in the operating theatre before the recipient's diseased organ is removed. The organ may have to be transported hundreds of kilometers—and speed is of the essence!

4   **Keeping Organs Fresh**

5   It is vitally important that the donor organs are kept healthy and functional once they have been removed from the donor's body. This is done by washing the blood out of them using special, chilled preservation fluid, which produces a state of "**suspended animation** (假死)" in the organ. This means the vital functions of the organ temporarily stop, but will return when the organ is connected to a bodily system again. They are stored in this fluid, surrounded by ice, to keep them at 4°C while they are transported to wherever they are needed. If ice actually came into

contact with the tissue, it would freeze it and cause permanent damage, and the organ would be of no use.

6 ### The Transplant Operation

7 Transplanting organs always involves surgery, and all surgery involves some risk to the patient. Firstly, the patient needs to be under an **anaesthetic** (*n.* 麻醉剂), in a chemically induced sleep while the operation takes place, so that he or she does not feel what is going on. It often takes a long time to carry out a transplant operation—several hours at least. The patient has to be carefully monitored to make sure there are no problems, and the risk of problems arising increases the longer the patient is under the anaesthetic.

8 Secondly, transplant surgery involves opening up the body to take out the old organ and replace it with a new one. As with all surgery, as soon as the body is opened up, it is easily infected. As the transplant surgery goes on for a long time, and involves introducing an organ from someone else's body, the risk is increased.

9 ### Transplant Challenges

10 Transplanting an organ raises some particular challenges. Each organ in the body carries out specific and very important functions. In many operations, the body of the patient continues as normal whilst surgery on a particular part goes on. During a transplant, entire organs are removed, and so their function may have to be taken over by machines. This is particularly true in heart and lung transplants, because the body cannot function without the oxygen they provide. The patient is often chilled, because at a low temperature the cells of the body need much less oxygen and sugar and they produce less waste. This means the cells are more likely to survive without any damage.

11 Another problem is making sure that the donor organ fits into the body of its new host. Obviously, transplants are only given when there will be a reasonable match between the size of the donor and the recipient, but even then there may still be problems. The original organ and the replacement will not be exactly the same, and neither will the blood **vessels** (*n.* 血管) that supply them with blood. Yet these blood vessels have to be joined together in such a way that they won't leak.

12 ### Rejection

13   The biggest fear of organ transplantation is that of **rejection** (*n.* 排异反应) —when the patient's immune system begins to recognize the new life—given organ —as foreign and tries to destroy it. It regards foreign cells—invading micro-organisms such as bacteria and viruses which might cause disease, and transplanted organs— as "non-self," which need to be destroyed. The immune system, which is so important in protecting the body against disease, is the worst enemy of a transplanted organ. The battle to prevent rejection has determined how successful transplant programs have been. After a transplant operation, a patient has to take a **cocktail** (*n.* 混合剂) of drugs every day for the rest of their life to prevent their immune system from destroying their new organ, because the body would never get used to the new organ and accept it.

(808 words)

Reading Comprehension

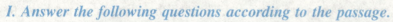

I. Answer the following questions according to the passage.

1. What is the function of the two teams before the transplanting operation?
2. How can the doctors keep the removed organ fresh?
3. What are the risks in the transplanting operation for the patient?
4. As to the body's function during an operation, what's the difference between transplantation and many other operations?
5. Why is there rejection after the organ transplantation?

II. Translate into Chinese the following sentences taken from the passage.

1. The tissue type of the donor must be matched as closely as possible with a person needing an organ transplant.
2. It is vitally important that the donor organs are kept healthy and functional once they have been removed from the donor's body.

3. The patient has to be carefully monitored to make sure there are no problems, and the risk of problems arising increases the longer the patient is under the anaesthetic.
4. Obviously, transplants are only given when there will be a reasonable match between the size of the donor and the recipient, but even then there may still be problems.
5. The immune system, which is so important in protecting the body against disease, is the worst enemy of a transplanted organ.

III. *Fill in the blanks with the words or phrases listed in Words and Expressions to Learn. Change the form where necessary.*

1. Pupils must be brought into _____ with new ideas.
2. China will _____ the 2008 Olympic Games.
3. Americans are likely to move many times in their lifetime; however, Chinese prefer to live in a place _____.
4. A terrible earthquake caused the total _____ of the town.
5. Something goes wrong with my computer _____.
6. Nothing has been settled down till now. The situation is still _____.
7. Since Sue is ill we'd better find a _____ for her.
8. The young man _____ his own life to save a drowning boy.
9. My uncle seems to be _____ to colds. He has never caught one.
10. The details were supposed to be secret but somehow _____ out.

Part IV Practical English

Business Correspondences(业务信函)(三)

介绍信是使本来不相识的人相互认识的一种信件,实质上恳请对方给予第三者以照顾和帮助。收信人从介绍信中可以了解到来者是什么人,要办什么事,有什么具体要求等。

介绍信一般包括以下的内容:
1. 明确交代介绍人与被介绍人之间的关系。
2. 交代被介绍人的姓名、身份等个人情况。
3. 此介绍信的原因、目的。
4. 对收信人的感谢。

介绍信可分私人介绍信和公务介绍信两种。

5. Personal Letters of Introduction

私人介绍信是写信人向自己的亲友介绍第三者,语气比较随便,格式与私人信函相同。

Sample

April 26, 2006

Dear Barbara,

    This letter will introduce my best friend Mary Brown of whom you've often heard me mention. She is going to be in Washington D. C. next month to lecture. I want very much to have her meet you there.

    And this seems like an excellent chance for you to meet each other. I think both of you will have a lot in common. So far as I know, you both are interested in modern literature. Once you meet her, you will really enjoy her company. Any kindness to her will be duly appreciated by me.

Yours affectionately,
(Signature)
Susan

亲爱的芭芭拉：

  特介绍我最好的朋友玛丽·布朗，你肯定经常听我说起她的。下个月她将去华盛顿特区参加一个讲座。我很想让她在那儿和你见一面。

  看来这可是你们俩相识的最佳时机。我认为你们有很多的相似之处。就我所知，你们都对现代文学感兴趣。只要你见着她，就一定会喜欢她的。如能给她提供任何帮助，我将不胜感激。

挚爱的

（签名）

苏珊

2006年4月26日

6. Official Letters of Introduction

  公务介绍信则是写信人因公把自己的同事、同学或业务关系人介绍给某单位或个人。这种介绍信语言和格式比较规范、严谨。公务介绍信称呼不知姓名者用 To Whom It May Concern，或 Dear Sir/Madam 相当于汉语的"敬启者"或"……（单位）负责同志"。

Sample

March 28, 2006

Dear Sir / Madam,

  This is to introduce Mr. Frank Jones, our new marketing manager, who will be in New York City from April 5 to April 9 on business.

  We shall appreciate it very much if you can provide the help Mr. Jones may need.

Yours faithfully,

(Signature)

Thomas Blank

President

Global Trading Inc., Los Angeles

151

敬启者：

    鄙公司新任业务经理弗兰克·琼斯先生将在四月五日至九日访问纽约。

    他在纽约期间如蒙惠助，不胜感激。

（签名）

托马斯·布莱克

洛杉矶全球贸易有限公司总裁

谨启

2006 年 3 月 28 日

Useful Expressions

1. This will introduce Mr. Fox to you.
   兹向您介绍弗克斯先生。

2. I am pleased to introduce Mr. Fox to you.
   我很乐意向您介绍弗克斯先生。

3. I take pleasure in introducing Mr. Fox to you.
   我很乐意向您介绍弗克斯先生。

4. I have the great pleasure of introducing Mr. Fox to you.
   我十分乐意把弗克斯先生介绍给贵方。

5. The bearer of this note, Mr. Fox, is entrusted with the task of establishing new business connection.
   兹介绍持信人弗克斯先生前往你处联系建立新商务关系事宜。

6. I am giving this letter to Mr. Fox, a good friend of mine, who is visiting Tokyo on May 1.
   兹介绍持信人，我的好友弗克斯先生，他将于 5 月 1 日去东京。

7. Please favor him with an interview.
   请予接洽为荷。

8. I shall be very grateful if you would do him some favor.
   如蒙帮助将不胜感激。

9. Thank you for the trouble I am causing you.
   给你添麻烦了，对此深表感谢。

10. Many thanks for the trouble you will have to take.
    烦劳之处，万分感激。

Writing Practice

I. Translate the following letter into Chinese.

April 15, 2006

Zhonghua Machinery Factory
Gentleman in Charge,

　　The bearer of this letter is Mr. Zhang Wen, who is entrusted with task of making the necessary arrangements with you for our students going to your factory for a visit.

　　Please favor him with an interview.

　　　　　　　　　　Academic Administration,
　　　　　　　　　　Dongfang University

II. Complete the following certificate according to the Chinese version.

August 8, 2006

Dear Sir,

　　(1) _____ （我们非常高兴向您介绍）Mr. Wang to you, our import manager of Textiles Department. Mr. Wang is spending three weeks in your city to (2) _____ （拓展商务）with chief manufacturers.

　　(3) _____ （我们将不胜感谢）if you will introduce him to reliable manufacturers and (4) _____ （向他提供所需的任何帮助或建议）.

　　　　　　　　　　　　　　　Yours faithfully,
　　　　　　　　　　　　　　　(Signature)
　　　　　　　　　　　　　　　John Smith

Part V English Salon

Auld Lang Syne

by Robert Burns

Should auld acquaintance be forgot,
And never brought to mind?
Should auld acquaintance be forgot,
And days of auld long syne?
And here's a hand, my trusty friend
And gie's a hand o' thine;
We'll take a cup o' kindness yet.
For auld lang syne.
For auld lang syne my dear,
For auld lang syne,
We'll take a cup o' kindness yet
For auld lang syne.

Notes

1. auld *adj.* (Scots) — old
   lang *adj.* (Scots) — long
   syne *adv.* (Scots) — since
   Auld Lang Syne — The Good Old Days
2. acquaintance 熟人
3. gie's — give us
4. o' thine — of yours

5. o'=of

 Requirement

Learn to sing and appreciate the song.

Unit Seven

Part I TEXT

Guide to Text-Learning

1. **Words and Expressions Related to the Topic**

aerobic	adj.	依靠氧气的;有氧健身法的
calory	n.	小卡路里;大卡路里
endorphins	n.	内啡肽 (a neurochemical occurring naturally in the brain and having analgesic properties)
fitness	n.	健康,结实
lung	n.	肺
cell	n.	【生物学】细胞
metabolism	n.	新陈代谢
monotonous	adj.	单调的,无变化的
rhythmic	adj.	节奏的;合拍的
session	n.	一段时间

2. **Grammatical Structures to Learn**

   (1) You can gradually **build up** from there.
   从那儿开始你就可以逐步增强体质。

   (2) You are **less prone to** over-use injuries that sometimes occur from doing the same exercise movements over and over again.
   不至于老是因过度锻炼而受到伤害,这正是由于不断采用同一运动方式而经常发生的。

   (3) You are also more likely to exercise **on a regular basis** and for longer periods of time.
   你也更有可能有规律地锻炼并且延长锻炼时间。

Warming-Up Questions:

1. What do you know about aerobic exercises?
2. Can you list some exercises connected with aerobic cross-training?
3. What kind of exercises do you usually do?

Aerobic Cross Training

1

The American College of Sports Medicine (ACSM) **defines** aerobic exercise as "any activity that uses large muscle groups, can be maintained continuously, and is rhythmic in nature." It is a type of exercise that **overloads** the heart and lungs and causes them to work harder than at rest. The important idea behind aerobic exercise today, is to get up and get moving! There are more activities than ever to choose from, whether it is a new activity or an old one. Find something you enjoy doing that keeps your heart rate **elevated** for a continuous time period and get moving to a healthier life.

2 Aerobic cross-training refers to using two to three different types of aerobic exercise during an exercise session. For example, if you plan to exercise for 60 minutes, you might start with 20 minutes of walking or jogging, followed by 20 minutes of biking, and finish with 20 minutes of rowing.

3 Now, please don't get the impression that you have to be in great shape to do this or that it has to be 60 minutes long. You can start with something as simple as a ten minute walk followed by ten minutes with an exercise video. This is cross-training too. You can gradually build up from there.

---

define /dɪˈfaɪn/ *v.*
state the precise meaning of (a word or sense of a word, for example); describe the nature or basic qualities of; explain
给……下定义;描述,解释

overload /ˈəʊvəˈləʊd/ *v.*
load too heavily
使超载,使过载

elevate /ˈelɪveɪt/ *v.*
move sth to a higher place or position from a lower one; lift
提高,提升

4   Here are some of the exercises you can use in your cross-training program; walking, jogging, biking, rowing, stair climbing, swimming, exercise **videos**, etc. Any **combination** of aerobic exercises will do. You simply go from one to the next with very little time between them.

5   Aerobic cross-training is beneficial to you in several ways:

6   1. It provides variety which **eliminates** the monotony often **associated** with doing the same exercise for a long period of time.

7   2. If your exercise sessions are less monotonous and more enjoyable, you are much more likely to exercise more often and for longer periods of time.

8   3. You are less prone to over-use injuries that sometimes occur from doing the same exercise movements over and over again.

9   4. You **tone** more muscles because you are using more muscles. For example, walking tones mostly the lower body muscles and rowing tones upper body muscles also. Even exercises like walking and biking that both tone lower body muscles, tone them at different **angles** and each tones some small muscles that the other doesn't.

10   5. Aerobic conditioning is very specific to the muscles being worked. For example, you can walk ten miles a day and still be somewhat breathless after climbing stairs because you haven't trained the muscles for that specific movement. Aerobic cross-training allows you to develop more comprehensive aerobic training.

11   6. Aerobic cross-training is effective for **weight** loss because you are toning and training the fat-burning systems of more of your muscles. It turns more of your muscles into 24-hour fat-burning machines! You are also more likely to exercise on a regular **basis** and for longer periods of time. This also **pro**

---

video /'vidiəu/ n.
visual portion of a televised broadcast; television
映像；电视

combination /ˌkɔmbi'neiʃən/ n.
the act of combining or the state of being combined
联合，合并

eliminate /i'limineit/ v.
get rid of; remove
消灭；消除

tone /təun/ v.
become stronger, brighter, more effective, etc.
增强

associate /ə'səuʃieit/ v.
connect or join together; combine
使发生联系，联合

angle /'æŋgl/ n.
the figure formed by two lines diverging from a common point; the place, position, or direction from which an object is presented to view
[数]角；视角

weight /weit/ n.
a measure of the heaviness of an object
重量

basis /'beisis/ n.
a foundation upon which sth rests
基础

motes weight loss and fitness.

12   Exercise doesn't have to be expensive to be effective. Any activity that raises the heart rate and is **maintained** for at least 20 minutes is considered aerobic. The best **workout routine** is one that you enjoy doing because you will continue to do something you enjoy. If you **vary** the different types of exercise it will help keep it fun and exciting. For the best results, do some type of aerobic cross-training activity at least 3 to 4 times a week.

12   Aerobic cross-training helps burn fat calories, increases your metabolism and if done on an empty stomach forces your body to recruit energy from stored fat cells. When you have finished your workout routine your metabolism will remain **elevating** for about 30 minutes. That means you continue to burn calories after you finish exercising.

13   If your goal is to control your weight, exercise your heart, **strengthen** your muscles or just feel healthier, a low-fat diet and regular aerobic cross-training activity will help you achieve and maintain a well toned and fit body. When you exercise the brain releases endorphins that put you in a better mood, make you feel happy and isn't that what life is all about?

(691 words)

---

promote /prə'məut/ v.
contribute to the progress or growth of
促进，推进

maintain /mein'tein/ v.
keep up or carry on; continue
维持或保持；继续

workout /'wə:kaut/ n.
the activity of exerting your muscles in various ways to keep fit
健身；体育锻炼

routine /ru:'ti:n/ n.
a prescribed, detailed course of action to be followed regularly; a standard procedure
例行公事；常规；日常事务；程序

vary /'veəri/ v.
make or cause changes in the characteristics or attributes of; modify or alter; give variety to; make diverse
变更，改变；使变化，使多样化

strengthen /'streŋθən/ v.
make strong or increase the strength of
加强

Useful Phrases

in nature	in fact	事实上
at rest	asleep; inactive; free from anxiety or distress	睡着了；静止的；不受焦虑或痛苦影响的
start with	have a beginning with	以……作为开始
build up	increase; develop; become larger; become stronger	增进；增大；增强
be prone to	having the probability of (usu. sth undesirable)	有……的倾向，易于
be less prone to	be not inclined to	不致老是……
on a... basis	(be done) in a... way; using a... method	在……基础上
on a regular basis	in a regular manner	定期地

1. Find something you enjoy doing that keeps your heart rate elevated for a continuous time period and get moving to a healthier life.

   找一些你喜欢的锻炼方法，让你的心脏在持续的一段时间内加快跳动起来，通过运动使你更加健康。

   本句中 that 引导的是分裂式定语从句，先行词为 something。由于先行词有别的修饰语，或者话语间插入了其他成分，或者为了强调等某种特殊的需要，定语从句和它修饰的先行词被分裂开了，这种现象叫做分裂式定语从句。例如：

   The professor is sleeping who has just come back from abroad after a long journey.

   刚刚长途跋涉从海外归来的教授正在睡觉。

2. It provides variety which eliminates the monotony often associated with doing the same exercise for a long period of time.

有氧交叉锻炼提供多样化的运动,避免了长时间单一运动的枯燥。

associated with 是过去分词短语作定语,修饰 monotony。过去分词短语作定语时,通常放在被修饰的名词之后,它的作用相当于一个定语从句。如:

This will be the best novel of its kind ever written (=that has ever been written).

这将是这类小说中写得最好的。

Who were the so-called guests invited (=who had been invited) to your party last night? 昨晚被邀请参加你的晚会的那些所谓的客人是谁呀?

3. You are also more likely to exercise on a regular basis and for longer periods of time. 你也就有可能定期地锻炼并且延长锻炼时间。

英语表示"非常可能"、"十有八九"等意思,可用 probable/probably 或 likely。注意,likely 既是形容词也是副词。probable 只能用在 It is probable that 的句型中,而不能说 We are probable to do sth。但 likely 既可用在 It is likely that...,也可用在 We are likely to do sth 的句型中。例如:

We are likely to make mistakes when learning English.

我们学英语时很可能犯错。

It is likely that she got soaked through in the rain.

她很可能被雨淋透了。

Reading Aloud and Memorizing the Following

I. Read the following paragraph taken from the text until you learn it by heart.

If your goal is to control your weight, exercise your heart, strengthen your muscles or just feel healthier, a low-fat diet and regular aerobic cross-training activity will help you achieve and maintain a well toned and fit body. When you exercise the brain releases endorphins that put you in a better mood, make you feel happy and isn't that what life is all about?

Comprehension of the Text

II. Choose the best answer to each of the following questions according to the passage.

1. What kind of mood can aerobic cross-training avoid?
   A. Sorrow.　　　B. Monotony.　　C. Happiness.　　D. Fear.
2. Aerobic cross-training can make you feel _____.
   A. monotonous　　B. hard　　C. enjoyable　　D. busy
3. Injuries may easily occur from doing _____.
   A. the same exercises　　　B. the different exercises
   C. aerobic cross-training　　D. the exercise
4. You tone more muscles when you _____.
   A. are biking　　　　　　　B. are walking
   C. are climbing the stairs　　D. are doing aerobic cross-training
5. If you want to control your weight, you'd better _____.
   A. be on a low fat diet　　　B. tone more muscles
   C. exercise your heart　　　 D. All above.

III. Answer the following questions with the information you've got from the text.
1. What is aerobic cross-training?   (Para. 2)
2. How do you begin your aerobic cross-training?   (Para. 3)
3. What kinds of exercises are easy for you to use in your cross-training program?   (Para. 4)
4. What part of muscles are you toning when climbing a mountain?   (Para. 9)
5. Why can you control your weight when doing aerobic exercises?   (Para. 12)

Vocabulary

IV. Spell out the words with the help of the given definitions and the first letters.
1. the usual food and drink of a person or animal (d _____)
2. get rid of (e _____)
3. a foundation upon which sth rests (b _____)
4. become stronger, brighter, more effective, etc. (t _____)
5. state the precise meaning of a word (d _____)
6. contribute to the progress or growth of (p _____)
7. connect or join together; combine (a _____)
8. a measure of the heaviness of an object (w _____)
9. load too heavily (o _____)
10. move (sth) to a higher place or position from a lower one (e _____)

V. Fill in the blanks with the words given below. Change the form where necessary.

| associate | basic | diet | elevate | eliminate |
| promote | routine | strength | vary | weight |

1. The fruit _____ the branches down.
2. I took the _____ to the eighteenth floor.
3. Their team was _____ in the first round.
4. The soldiers _____ their defenses.
5. They are working for the _____ of the world peace.
6. For _____ reasons I'd prefer not to meet him.
7. We drew this conclusion on the _____ of experiments.
8. Proper _____ and exercise are both important for health.

9. There has always been a close _____ between these two schools.
10. She found it difficult to establish a new _____ after retirement.

VI. Fill in the blanks with proper prepositions or adverbs.

1. It is one of the strangest things _____ nature.
2. In this chapter we will start _____ a very simple kind of electric device—an electric torch.
3. This regulation refers only _____ children.
4. Fresh air is beneficial _____ our health.
5. The disease occurs most frequently _____ rural areas.
6. It turns more of your muscles _____ 24-hour fat-burning machines!
7. He's prone _____ minor illnesses.
8. _____ the basis of our sales forecasts, we may begin to make a profit next year.
9. You can keep your mind _____ rest about the matter, it's all set.
10. Every morning he spent two hours training _____ the race.

Structure

VII. Rewrite the following sentences after the models.

Model 1 You can gradually **make yourself stronger** from there.
You can gradually **build up** from there.

1. She was studying to develop her math.
2. I can't work up any interest in this book.
3. The soldiers strengthened their defenses.
4. Eventually, these books will accumulate into a fine library.
5. Promote physical culture and tone up the people's health.

Model 2 You **have a (less/more) tendency to** over-use injuries that sometimes occur from doing the same exercise movements over and over again...
You **are (less/more) prone to** over-use injuries that sometimes occur from doing the same exercise movements over and over again...

1. People are more possible to make mistakes when they are tired.

2. I'm inclined to believe he's innocent.
3. He had a tendency to shrink up whenever attention was focused on him.
4. Generally speaking, I'm inclined to agree with you.
5. Children of good health are less possible to catch colds in winter.

VIII. Study the model and translate the following sentences into English, using the phrase "on ... basis."

Model: You are also more likely to exercise **on a regular basis** and for longer periods of time.

1. 记住定期做这件事。
2. 这间办公室不必每天做清洁。
3. 这些人在自愿的基础上献血。
4. 实验结果是在每天检验的基础上获得的。
5. 邀请大家自愿提供信息。

Translation

IX. Translate the following sentences into Chinese.

1. The important idea behind aerobic exercise today is to get up and get moving!

2. For example, if you plan to exercise for 60 minutes, you might start with 20 minutes of walking or jogging, followed by 20 minutes of biking, and finish with 20 minutes of rowing.

3. Aerobic conditioning is very specific to the muscles being worked.

4. Aerobic cross-training is effective for weight loss because you are toning and training the fat-burning systems of more of your muscles.

5. Any activity that raises the heart rate and is maintained for at least 20 minutes is considered aerobic.

X. Translate the following sentences into English using the words or phrases in the brackets.

1. BP 机到 21 世纪就逐渐被淘汰了。(eliminate)

2. 很难解释清楚到底发生了什么变化。(define)

3. 运动使肌肉强化。(tone)

4. 我不愿再和他们交往了。(associate)

5. 她的话使我放心。(at rest)

Part II Grammar

Subordinate Clauses(从句)(二)

从句(二)状语从句(Adverbial Clauses)

用作状语的分句结构叫做状语从句。状语从句可以位于主句之前,也可位于主句之后。状语从句在句子中充当副词的作用,因此在句子中可以表示时间、地点、原因、条件、目的、结果、比较、让步、方式等。

1. 时间状语从句

通常由以下连词引导:when, whenever, as, while, since, until, till, after, before, as soon as, no sooner... than..., hardly (scarcely)... when 等。例如:

When you have finished your workout routine your metabolism will remain elevated for about 30 minutes.
在完成了日常锻炼后,你的新陈代谢还会持续旺盛30分钟。

I'd like to see you **whenever** it's convenient.
在你方便的时候我想来看看你。

That means you continue to burn calories **after** you finish exercising.
那意味着在锻炼后热量燃烧还在继续。

Hardly had the game begun **when** it started raining.
比赛刚刚开始就下起雨来。

2. 地点状语从句

通常由连词 where, wherever 引导。例如:

Put it **where** we can all see it.
把它放在我们都看得见的地方。

Wherever she goes, there are crowds of people waiting to see her.
她所到之处都有成群的人等着见她。

3. 原因状语从句

最常用的连词有 because, since, as, 还有 now (that) 和 seeing (that)。例如：

The best workout routine is one that you enjoy doing **because** you will continue to do something you enjoy.

你最喜欢的运动就是最好的常规健身，因为喜欢，你才能持之以恒。

Since you can't answer the question, you'd better ask someone else.

既然你无法回答这个问题，你最好再问问别人。

As you weren't there I left a message.

因为你不在那里，我留了个信儿。

Seeing (that) the weather is bad, we'll stay at home.

因为天气不好，我们要呆在家里了。

在 because, since, as 中，because 直接回答 why 提问的问句，语气最强；since 表示众所周知的且业已存在的原因；as 的语气最弱；now (that) 和 seeing that 引导原因状语从句时，常放在句首。

4. 目的状语从句

常用的连词有 so that, in order that, that, in case 等。其中 in case 用于非正式文体中。例如：

She simplified the instructions **so that** the children could understand them.

她简化了指令以便于儿童理解。

My father works hard **in order that** he may support us.

为了养家我父亲辛苦地工作。

5. 条件状语从句

常用的连词有 if, unless, suppose, in case, provided (that), so long as, but that 等。例如：

If you vary the different types of exercise it will help keep it fun and exciting.

如果采用不同的锻炼方式，那将有助于你保持对运动的兴趣和激动。

Unless England improves their game they're going to lose the match.

英格兰队如果不改进打法，就会输掉这场比赛。

I will come **provided that** I am well enough.

只要我身体好一定来。

We can arrange everything **so long as** we have enough time.

只要有足够的时间,我们就能安排一切。

6. 让步状语从句

常用的连词有 though, although, even if (though), as, no matter+if 或 wh- 疑问词结构..., whatever (whoever, however,...)。例如:

I don't know him well **though** I've known him for a long time.

我对他并不了解,虽然我认识他已经很长时间了。

We should practice economy **even** if we are rich.

即使我们富裕了也仍应该厉行节约。

Day in, day out, **no matter** what the weather is like, she walks ten miles.

她不管天气如何,每天总是步行十英里。

Whatever I say, he always disagrees.

不管我说什么,他总是不同意。

7. 结果状语从句

常用的连词有 so... that, so that, such... that。例如:

The term and condition are printed in very small letters **so that** they are difficult to read.

条款与条件是用很小的字体印刷的,以致难以阅读。

The mountain is **so** high **that** she can't climb it up to the top.

那座山太高了,她无法登上山顶。

It was **such** a warm day **(that)** we all took off our overcoats when we climbed up the mountain.

天气这么好,我们在登山时都把外衣脱了。

8. 比较状语从句

常用的连词有 as... as, not so (not as 或 not such)...as, ...than。

My brother is **more** experienced in this **than** I (am).

我兄弟在这方面比我有经验。

This problem is **not so** easy to solve **as** you imagine.

这个问题并非你所想象的那么容易解决。

9. 方式状语从句

常用的连词有 as, as if (though) 等。例如：

He speaks English almost **as** a native speaker does.

他的英文几乎说得和以英语为母语的人一样。

He behaves **as if** he had no common sense.

他的言行就好像没有常识似的。

I. Complete each of the following sentences with the most appropriate word or words from the four choices marked A, B, C and D.

1. _____ we got to the station, the train had left already.
   A. If   B. Unless   C. Since   D. When

2. I'll stay here _____ everyone else comes back.
   A. even if   B. as though   C. because   D. till

3. Although it's raining, _____ are still working in the field.
   A. they   B. but they   C. and they   D. so they

4. You'll miss the train _____ you hurry up.
   A. unless   B. as   C. if   D. until

5. When you read the book, you'd better make a mark _____ you have any questions.
   A. at which B. at where   C. the place   D. where

6. We'd better hurry _____ it is getting dark.
   A. and   B. but   C. as   D. unless

7. I didn't manage to do it _____ you had explained how.
   A. until   B. unless   C. when   D. before

8. I hurried _____ I wouldn't be late for class.
   A. since   B. so that   C. as if   D. unless

9. Helen listened carefully _____ she might discover exactly what she needed.
   A. in that   B. in order that C. in case   D. even though

10. Small _____ it is, the pen is a most useful tool.
   A. because   B. so   C. if   D. as

II. Fill in the blanks with the words given.

| so that | whatever | how | until | although |
| as if | the more | before | as | since |

1. No matter _____ hard it may be I will carry it out.
2. The earth goes round the sun just _____ the moon goes round the earth.
3. He must practise often _____ he can speak fluently.
4. She acted _____ nothing had happened.
5. I had gone abroad _____ you came to see me last year.
6. Don't go away _____ I come back.
7. I don't believe him, _____ he says.
8. _____ he worked all day, he couldn't finish the job.
9. _____ you are free tonight, why not drop in and play chess with me?
10. The more he explained, _____ I was puzzled.

Part III Reading Practice

Guide to Reading

1. Words and Expressions to Learn

approach	v.	接近；动手处理
barrier	n.	(阻碍通道的)障碍物
defense	n.	防御
derive	v.	得自，起源
emphasis	n.	强调
breach	n.	违背；破坏
intensity	n.	强烈，剧烈；强度
media	n.	媒体
mimic	v.	模仿
profound	adj.	深刻的，意义深远的
provocation	n.	激怒；刺激；挑衅；挑拨
reward	v.	酬劳，奖赏
terrorism	n.	恐怖主义；恐怖统治；恐怖行动
victorious	adj.	获胜的，胜利的
yell	v.	叫喊，叫嚷
root for	v.	全力支持；赞助；为……加油喝彩
make a goal		得一分
get mad		发脾气
make sure		弄明白(查明白)
become accustomed to		习惯于
knock out		敲出；击倒；打破；打落

2. Pre-Reading Questions

(1) Have you ever meet with sports violence?

(2) What do you think of sports violence?

Sports Violence

—A Danger to Us All

1   People all over the world enjoy watching sports matches. We all love rooting for our favorite teams and cheering whenever they make a goal, get a hit, score a point, or are otherwise victorious. Sports can be a great way to relax or to have fun, and it is enjoyed by the young and old alike. However, we have also seen times when sports are not the greatest influence. Sometimes sports players get mad at each other.  They will often yell angry words at each other, and sometimes they will even get violent and hit each other. There have even been a couple of times where people have died in sports violence.

2   **Physical vs. Violent**

3   Sports are very physical activities. They require our bodies to be in great shape, and reward us for being strong and healthy. Sports are a great way to let our physical strengths be used for something positive (*adj.* 积极的). Violence, however, uses the same physical strengths, but uses them to do harm to other people. We should make sure that even as we improve our bodies through sports, we never use that power to hurt others.

173

4 **A Bad Influence**

5 We need to make sure that we never get violent with other people, but those sports stars who get in fights should also be ashamed. Many very young people watch sports matches, and some of those sports stars are those youths' heroes. If they see their favorite sports star yelling and beating someone up, they will think that it is Ok to do those types of things. With increasing amounts of violence in sports today our children are becoming more and more accustomed to it. With the media's influence, our society has grown to **appreciate** (*v.* 赏识) and encourage **misbehavior** (*n.* 不良行为) in athletic events. Our children of today look to athletes as role models and have begun to mimic their violent trends. With the emphasis on winning and the **overflowing** (*n.* 泛滥) emotions in athletic competition it is essential that we encourage good **sportsmanship** (*n.* 运动员精神), positive attitudes, and reminders that winning isn't everything. We need to do our best to stop sports violence to make sure these sports players are not being a bad influence on the world's children.

6 **Fan Behavior**

7 To no surprise, the fans came to their player's defense much like the player's teammates did. "However, what is interesting is the league's reaction to the players' retaliation. I'm not sure what message they're sending to fans if their **instigation** (*n.* 鼓动, 煽动) and **provocation** (*n.* 激怒, 刺激) can essentially knock out the best players on the opposing team for half or all of the season." Hirt is particularly interested in the feelings and behavior of sports fans. His research has focused on the reasons why fans have such profound **allegiances** (*n.* 效忠) to various teams and players and what they derive from this association.

8 Research into fan behavior, fan influence on players and player influence on fans suggests that players are not significantly influenced by fan behavior, but fans are influenced by the behavior of players, said Lynn Jamieson, professor and chairman of the Department of Recreation and Park Administration in Indiana University Bloomington's School of Health, Physical Education and Recreation. The **brawling** (*n.* 吵架) at the Pacers-Pistons game raises the issue of players breaking through the imaginary barrier between the player/contest area and the fan area. This breach, she said, has been similar in other less violent events in

recent years, such as when players approach cheering fans during games to receive their enthusiastic praise, but this is really "a first" for player-to-fan violence in terms of its **intensity** (*n.* 强度) and lack of control. Sports "tend to reflect society," said Jamieson, whose research interests include sport, terrorism and violence. "We have a violent society where people use violence to solve problems."

9   **In Our Own Neighborhood**

10   The next time you are playing a sport, make sure that everyone is playing fairly. Remind people the goal is not to hurt each other, it's just to have fun and try our best. When we are watching a game, we can also make sure that we do not support players who are continuously violent. We need to show them that sports violence is wrong, and not supporting it is the best way.

(716 words)

Reading Comprehension

I. Answer the following questions according to the passage.

1. Why do we like to watch sports matches?
2. How does violence use physical strengths?
3. What influence does sports violence give to many young people?
4. What problem does the brawling at the Pacers-Pistons game raise?
5. What attitude should we have to play a sport?

II. Translate into Chinese the following sentences taken from the passage.

1. We all love rooting for our favorite teams and cheering whenever they make a goal, get a hit, score a point, or are otherwise victorious.
2. We should make sure that even as we improve our bodies through sports, we never use that power to hurt others.

3. With the emphasis on winning and the overflowing emotions in athletic competition it is essential that we encourage good sportsmanship, positive attitudes, and reminders that winning isn't everything.
4. We have a violent society where people use violence to solve problems.
5. When we are watching a game, we can also make sure that we do not support players who are continuously violent.

III. Fill in the blanks with the words or phrases listed in Words and Expressions to Learn. Change the form where necessary.

1. The time is _____ when we must think about buying a new house.
2. Our professor is a man of _____ learning.
3. _____ is a threat to the whole country.
4. Poor health may be a _____ to success.
5. To _____ that he was at home, I called him up in advance.
6. It was a happy day when our football team was _____.
7. John was _____ the Scottish football team in the World Cup.
8. Some schools put great _____ on language study.

Part IV　Practical English

Business Correspondences（业务信函）（四）

7. Letters of Recommendation

推荐信可能直接关系到申请人能否获得所申请的职位，能否出国留学并获得奖学金等。推荐信的目的是向对方介绍申请人的工作、学习和能力等方面的情况。推荐信一般应包括下列内容：

被推荐人的基本情况介绍；推荐人对被推荐人的基本评价；推荐信尾必须有推荐人的亲笔签名。

推荐信经常使用一些褒奖的形容词来描述被推荐人。以下是一些常用的描述品行和能力的词语：bright, clever, capable, gifted, talented, out-standing, prominent, diligent, industrious, conscientious, hardworking, self-motivated, eager to learn, quick-minded, quick-witted, strong-minded, open-minded, humorous, good-humored, cooperative, compromising, competent, ambitious, creative, original, innovative, inventive, imaginative, firm, persistent, persevering, resourceful, kind-hearted, generous, honest, helpful, cheerful, considerate, devoted, dedicated, committed, promising, far beyond the average person 等。

推荐信开头的称呼，可以泛泛地用 To Whom It May Concern（敬启者），不涉及具体的人或单位，其好处是可以一式数份，同时寄给几个学校或单位。

(1) 求职推荐信 (Letters of Recommendation for a Position)

Sample

Jan. 3rd, 1997

Dear Ms. Brown:

   Mr. Lewis Lee worked as product manager in this company for three years, from 1993 to 1996. This warm-hearted gentleman took up the responsibility during the whole period.

   Mr. Lee has a combination of excellent qualities. He is one of the top brilliant and entertaining employees I have ever met. Frankly saying, he is a gold mine to whoever employs him.

   Because of the reasons listed above, I recommend Mr. Lee without reservation.

Yours sincerely,
(Signature)
Thomas Smith

尊敬的布朗女士：

　　刘易斯·李先生从1993年起，在我公司任产品部经理一职至1996年。这位热心的先生在整个任职期间忠于职守。

　　李先生具有许多难以兼得的优点。他是我遇到过的职员中最有智慧和最令人愉快的几个人之一。坦白地讲，他对任何一个雇主都是一笔难得的财富。

　　由于以上提到的理由，我毫无保留地推荐李先生。

　　此致

（签名）
托马斯·史密斯
1997年1月3日

(2) 留学推荐信 (Letters of Recommendation for Study Abroad)

Sample

To Whom It May Concern:

I have the pleasure of writing this letter of recommendation for Mr. Wang Shengli, who is a student of mine. He wishes to be considered an applicant for the MS course of physics at your college.

Mr. Wang is a gifted young man. He has devoted his heart to his study and research. Not only has he obtained As in all major subject areas, but he has also published several articles in the school journal, illustrating his originality and his deep understanding of science. For his competence, creativeness, and persistence, he is respected by everyone who knows him.

I feel sure that, if he is accepted by your college, he will be able to develop his talent to its fullest potential. I sincerely hope you will give him favorable consideration.

         Yours cordially,
          (Signature)
         Luo Dongliang
    Professor of Physics, Shanghai University of Technology

敬启者：

  我很高兴为我的学生王胜利先生写这封推荐信。他申请攻读贵校物理专业硕士学位。

  王先生是一个很有天赋的小伙子，他全身心地扑在学习和研究上，不仅所有主要课程都得 A 级，而且在校刊上发表了好几篇文章，这些文章都显示了他的独创性和对科学的深刻理解。由于他的才华、创造性和坚韧精神，了解他的人都很尊敬他。

  我深信，如果贵校录取他的话，他将能够把自己潜在的才华充分挖掘出来。我诚挚地希望贵校能优先考虑他的申请。

           罗栋梁　谨上
            （签名）
            物理学教授
            上海理工大学

Writing Practice

Complete the following Letter of Recommendation according to the Chinese version.

敬启者：
　　我荣幸地推荐陆盛楠先生到贵银行任职。
　　陆先生为人正直，办事一丝不苟，工作效率高，在我银行担任高级出纳员五年有余，有口皆碑。
　　自从我国加入世贸组织以来，越来越多的海外银行在上海开设分行。陆先生希望能够到这样一家银行工作，以求更好的个人发展。
　　我很舍不得他离开，但是为了他的前途和上海的发展，我极力推荐他到贵银行工作。

　　　　　　　　　　　　　　　　　　　　　　　　　　　董为华　谨上
　　　　　　　　　　　　　　　　　　　　　　　　　　　　（签名）
　　　　　　　　　　　　　　　　　　　　　　　　　　上海建设银行经理

To Whom It May __1__,

　　It is my __2__ to recommend Mr. Lu Shengnan for a position in your esteemed bank.

　　A man of integrity, meticulousness, and __3__, Mr. Lu has worked as a senior teller in my bank for over five years and won public praise among his colleagues.

　　Ever since China's entry to WTO, more and more overseas banks have established branches in Shanghai. Mr. Lu hopes to work in one of these branches for a better prospect.

　　I am sorry to lose him but, for his own good __4__ for the development of Shanghai, I highly __5__ him to you.

　　　　　　　　　　　　　　　　　　　　Yours cordially,
　　　　　　　　　　　　　　　　　　　　(Signature)
　　　　　　　　　　　　　　　　　　　　Dong Weihua
　　　　　　　　　　　　　　　　　　　　Manager, Shanghai Construction Bank

Part V   English Salon

Learn to Sing the Following English Song

Big Big World

I'm a big big girl
In a big big world.
It's not a big big thing if you leave me,
But I do do feel
That I too too will miss you much,
Miss you much... (To be repeated)

I can see the first leaf falling.
It's all yellow and nice.
It's so very cold outside
Like the way I'm feeling inside.

(Repeat the first paragraph)

Outside it's now raining,
And tears are falling from my eyes.
Why did it have to happen?
Why did it all have to end?

(Repeat the first paragraph)

I have your arms around me ooooh like fire,
But when I open my eyes,
You're gone...

(Repeat the first paragraph twice)

Unit Eight

Part I TEXT

Guide to Text-Learning

1. *Words and Expressions Related to the Topic*

environmentalist	环保主义者
economy	经济
economist	经济学家
trend	趋势
span	持续时间
explosion	爆炸
disaster	大灾难
cattle	牛；家畜
breakthrough	突破
tumor	肿瘤
CAT scans	计算机化 x 射线轴向分层扫描
tuberculosis	肺结核
spill	（液体）洒出，泼出

2. *Grammatical Structures to Learn*

   (1) But the fast development of world economy will **bring about** many new problems.
   但是，世界经济的快速发展将带来许多新问题。

   (2) **Using fossil fuels for energy** has not altered very much but wind energy use is increasing significantly.
   以矿物燃料为能源的情况没有发生多大变化，但是对风力的利用越来越受到重视。

183

(3) People seem to have forgotten ways to **keep** diseases **under control**.
人们似乎已忘记控制疾病的方法。

> *Warming-Up Questions:*
> 1. Our environment is being polluted, what can we students do to prevent it?
> 2. Can we develop our economy at the cost of our environment?
> 3. Is there an energy crisis all over the world? Give some examples.

Trends for the 21st Century

1 What problems will our world encounter in the next 1,000 years? Social scientists and economists, farming experts and environmentalists **pose** this question and examine data, information from **surveys**.

2 In every field, experts examine changes to understand the state of the field. To understand a country's economy, economists check growth in an industry such as steel. To understand the state of business, they may look at the number of building permits for new houses. The information learned shows increases or decreases. Important trends **emerge** in each field.

3 **Population**

4 Population is important to every person on earth. People tend to live longer in most places. In central Europe, however, life span is dropping because health care is not what it was a few years ago. Factors affecting general health include **excessive** smoking and drinking of alcohol and polluted water supplies.

5 The population explosion on our planet has been increasing at an alarming rate but the

---

pose /pəuz/ v.
raise a question (esp. one that needs serious thought)
提问，质询

survey /səː'vei/ n.
investigation
调查

emerge /i'məːdʒ/ v.
come out of a dark, enclosed or hidden place
（从暗处）出现

excessive /ik'sesiv/ adj.
greater than what seems reasonable or appropriate
过度的，过分的

percentage of increase is decreasing. One out of every five people on earth is Chinese, yet China's growth rate has slowed down. As the number of women going to school increases, the growth rate **declines**.

6 **Food Production**

7 The production of grain seems to be decreasing mainly because of climate changes. Natural disasters like storms and floods have washed away many crops.

8 With less land for cattle and sheep, less meat like beef and lamb is being produced. Production of chicken, turkey and fish has increased, however. The amount of ocean fish has not increased, but fish farm production has.

9 Fish farming is very **efficient**: producing a kilogram of fish **utilizes** less than 2 kilograms of feed, but it takes 2.2 kilograms of feed to produce 1 kilogram of chicken. One kilogram of beef requires 7 kilograms of grain. People, therefore, may eat less red meat in the future and more fish.

10 **Energy**

11 Using fossil fuels for energy has not **altered** very much but wind energy use is increasing **significantly**. Energy from nuclear power plants is **steadily** increasing but the problem of dangerous waste limits its growth in many regions. Because many electrical companies consider nuclear energy too expensive, the trend is toward less dangerous sources of energy.

12 While natural gas use increases, use of coal as fuel is decreasing. Natural gas, an **outstanding** energy fuel, can be used to heat homes, make electricity, and power cars.

13 **Economics**

14 As countries around the world trade more with one another, more products are available. But the fast development of world economy will bring about many new problems. With fewer trees, the paper industry is producing more paper from

---

decline /dɪˈklaɪn/ v.
decrease
下降

efficient /ɪˈfɪʃənt/ adj.
having efficiency
高效的

utilize /ˈjuːtɪlaɪz/ v.
make use of
利用

alter /ˈɔːltə/ v.
become different; to make sth/sb different
(使)变动,更改

significantly /sɪgˈnɪfɪkəntli/ adv.
in a way that is large or important enough to have an effect on sth
有重大意义地,显著地

steadily /ˈstedɪli/ adv.
(development, growth) gradually and in an even and regular way
(发展,增长等)稳步地,持续地

outstanding /aʊtˈstændɪŋ/ adj.
excellent, extremely good
杰出的,优秀的

recycled materials but, unfortunately, damages the planet. The paper-making process uses large amounts of water, burns fossil fuels and produces much chemical waste.

15   Automobile production is down; bicycle production is up. Crowded highways, high gasoline costs, and ease of bicycling are three reasons for the change.

16   **Health**

17   Three major health trends exist as we begin the new century. Health care is better than ever. Medical research breakthroughs include finding tumors early, and saving lives through CAT scans and surgery. Surviving cancer is a new trend. HIV/AIDS, however, is spreading quickly all over the world.

18   The third major trend is toward an attitude of **indifference**. People seem to have forgotten ways to keep diseases under control. Although medical science had **achieved** control over several dangerous diseases, some are returning. For instance, tuberculosis, once a dangerous killer, was **cured**. Now the disease is appearing again.

19   **Nature**

20   Pollution continues to affect our forests and water. The bird population is decreasing because of oil spills and spreading cities. Seas and oceans are changing. Trees are cut down, more soil is washed away, and water quality is affected. Many of these trees are in our rain forests where thick areas of plants and trees, home for many birds and animals, are disappearing.

21   **Conclusion**

22   Our challenges for this new century are clear. The problems of **numerous inhabitants** on this small planet will continue to be important to each of us. These

---

recycle /ˈriːˈsaikl/ v.
treat things been used so that they can be used again
回收利用

indifference /inˈdifrəns/ n.
a lack of interest, feeling or reaction toward sb/sth
漠不关心, 冷淡

achieve /əˈtʃiːv/ v.
succeed in doing
成功完成

cure /kjuə/ v.
(sb or sth) make a person or animal healthy again after an illness
治愈

numerous /ˈnjuːmərəs/ adj.
(formal) existing in large numbers
许多的

inhabitant /inˈhæbitənt/ n.
a person or animal living in a particular place
居民; 栖息动物

challenges show that all of us need to be **involved** in solving the problems. May we find new ways to accomplish the task?

> involve /ɪnˈvɒlv/ v.
> be affected by or taken part in
> 牵涉;参加

(683words)

Useful Phrases ▶▶▶ ▶▶▶

tend to do	be likely to do sth or happen	往往会,总是
at an alarming rate	at a surprising speed	以惊人的速度
wash away	(of water) remove or carry sb/sth away	冲掉,冲走
keep... under control	deal with successfully	把……控制住
be involved in	be affected or taken part in	卷入其中,牵涉

Notes

1 To understand the state of business, they may look at the number of building permits for new houses. 为了了解行业的状况,他们可能会调查新房建造许可证的发放数量。
To understand... 不定式短语在此用作目的状语。

2 Factors affecting general health include excessive smoking and drinking of alcohol and polluted water supplies. 影响大众健康的因素包括吸烟过度、酗酒以及饮水污染。
affecting general health 是一个现在分词短语,在此用作后置定语,修饰 factors。

3 People seem to have forgotten ways to keep diseases under control. 人们似乎已忘了如何控制疾病。
... to have forgotten 不定式使用了完成式,表明不定式动作先于谓语动词发生。

187

4 ... numerous inhabitants on this small planet... 生活在这个小行星上的无数居民

on this small planet 介词短语在此作后置定语。

Exercises

Reading Aloud and Memorizing the Following

I. Read aloud the following paragraph taken from the text until you learn it by heart.

  Pollution continues to affect our forests and water. The bird population is decreasing because of oil spills and spreading cities. Seas and oceans are changing. Trees are cut down, more soil washes away, and water quality is affected. Many of these trees are in our rain forests where thick areas of plants and trees, home for many birds and animals, are disappearing.

Comprehension of the text

II. Choose the best answer to each of the following questions according to the passage.

1. What problems will our world encounter in the next 1,000 years?
   A. Industry, economics, nature, housing, economics, nature, employment.
   B. Food production, employment, population, health, economics, nature.
   C. Health, economics, nature, housing, economics, nature, employment.
   D. Population, food production, energy, health, economics, nature.
2. Experts examine changes _____.
   A. to understand the state of the field
   B. to understand a country's economy
   C. to solve those problems
   D. to guide industry production

3. In central Europe, however, life span is _____.
   A. increasing   B. longer
   C. going up   D. going down
4. Why may people eat more fish in the future?
   A. Because fish need less feed.
   B. Because fish grow quickly.
   C. Because people like eating fish.
   D. Because fish is healthy food.
5. What continues to affect our forests and water?
   A. Population.   B. The bird population.
   C. Seas and oceans.   D. Pollution.

III. Answer the following questions with the information you've got from the text.

1. Why does life span drop in central Europe? (Para. 4)
2. Why can't we eat more red meat in the future? (Para. 9)
3. What's the problem with nuclear energy? (Para. 11)
4. What causes automobile production down and bicycle up? (Para. 15)
5. What are the three major trends about health? (Para. 17, 18)

Vocabulary

IV. Spell out the words with the help of the given definitions and the first letters.

1. come out of a dark, enclosed place (e _____)
2. use again (r _____)
3. make use of (u _____)
4. excellent (o _____)
5. accomplish (a _____)
6. investigation (s _____)
7. extreme (e _____)
8. change (a _____)
9. decrease (d _____)
10. many (n _____)

V. Fill in the blanks with the words given below. Change the form where necessary.

| available | excessive | alter | achieve | indifference |
| significant | efficient | utilize | decline | tend |

1. The government can't afford to be _____ to public opinion.
2. Its findings provide the scientific foundation for rational _____ of land.
3. The new drug has great _____ for the treatment of the disease.
4. Tickets are _____ free of charge for the school.
5. I was impressed by the _____ with which she handled the crisis.
6. Are you suffering from an _____ of stress in your life?
7. His illness grew out of his _____ to overwork.
8. An increase in cars has resulted in the _____ of public transport.
9. They're making some _____ to the house.
10. Flying across the Atlantic for the first time was a great _____.

VI. Fill in the blanks with proper prepositions or adverbs.

1. The sun emerged _____ behind the cloud.
2. The doctor cured him _____ his cancer.
3. He had finally managed to break _____ his fear.
4. The table takes _____ too much room.
5. There is a growing trend _____ earlier retirement.
6. Parts of the path had been washed _____ by the sea.
7. The European Union has set strict limits _____ levels of pollution.
8. We need to cut the article _____ to 1,000 words.
9. We encourage students to study _____ their own pace.
10. People complain that prices of houses are going _____ rapidly these days.

Structure

VII. Rewrite or complete the following sentences after the models.

Model 1   But the fast development of world economy will **cause** many new problems.

> But the fast development of world economy will **bring about** many new problems.

1. She made various efforts to make a peaceful solution of the problem.
2. He caused a quarrel between his parents.
3. Scientists say that many factors produce changes in the weather.
4. You could only begin Mary's misery.
5. The Second World War was produced by Hitler's invasion of Poland.

Model 2 Surviving cancer (治好癌症) is a new trend.

1. _____ (不准时) makes him unreliable.
2. _____ (敲钟) marked the end of the old year.
3. _____ (用慢火煮) makes tough meat tender.
4. _____ (与他们争吵) is a waste of time.
5. _____ (迷路) can be a terrifying experience.

VIII. Study the model and translate the following sentences into English, using the phrase "keep under control."

Model: People seem to have forgotten ways to **keep** diseases **under control**.

1. 我国政府控制了禽流感。
2. 便衣警察们被告知要控制那个嫌疑人。
3. 大火终于被控制住了。
4. 这个调皮的男孩需要管教。
5. 他再也不能控制住自己的感情了。

Translation

IX. Translate the following sentences into Chinese.

1. The production of grain seems to be decreasing mainly because of climate changes. Natural disasters like storms and floods have washed away many crops.

2. Energy from nuclear power plants is steadily increasing but the problem of dangerous waste limits its growth in many regions.

3. Social scientists and economists, farming experts and environmentalists pose this question and examine data, information from surveys.

4. The third major trend is toward an attitude of indifference. People seem to have forgotten ways to keep diseases under control.

5. Surviving cancer is a new trend. HIV/AIDS, however, is spreading quickly all over the world.

X. *Translate the following sentences into English. using the words or phrases in the brackets.*

1. 在医疗改革的过程中,我们遇到了来自各方面的阻力。(encounter)

2. 所有能找到的专家都被召集到了现场。(available)

3. 他变得我几乎认不出来了。(alter)

4. 他们的家庭背景使他们很难有机会在社会上取得成就。(achieve)

5. 消防员花了两个小时才把火势控制住。(keep... under control)

Part II Grammar

Subordinate Clauses(从句)(三)

从句(三)定语从句(Adverbial Clauses)

可用于修饰名词、代词或名词性结构的句子称为定语从句。被修饰的名词、词组或代词即先行词。定语从句通常出现在先行词之后,由关系代词 who, whom, whose, that, which 等或关系副词 when, where, why 等引出。

1. 关系代词引导的定语从句

关系代词所代替的先行词是人或物的名词或代词,并在句中充当主语、宾语、定语等成分。关系代词在定语从句中作主语时,从句谓语动词的人称和数要和先行词保持一致。

who, whom, that 这些词代替的先行词是人的名词或代词；whose 用来指人或物(只用作定语)；若指物,可换为 of which; which, that 所代替的先行词是事物的名词或代词,在从句中可作主语、宾语等。例如：

They rushed over to help the man whose car had broken down.
那人的车坏了,大家都跑过去帮忙。

Please pass me the book whose (of which) cover is green.
请递给我那本绿皮的书。

A prosperity which / that had never been seen before appears in the countryside.
农村出现了前所未有的繁荣。

The package (which / that) you are carrying is about to come unwrapped.
你拿的包快散了。

2. 关系副词引导的定语从句

关系副词可代替的先行词是表示时间、地点或理由的名词,在从句中作状语。

关系副词 when, where, why 的含义相当于"介词＋which"结构,因此常常和"介词＋which"结构交替使用,例如：

There are occasions when (on which) one must yield.

任何人都有不得不屈服的时候。

Beijing is the place where (in which) I was born.

北京是我的出生地。

Is this the reason why (for which) he refused our offer?

这就是他拒绝我们帮助他的理由吗?

His father died the year when (in which) he was born.

他父亲在他出生那年去世了。

He is unlikely to find the place where (in which) he lived forty years ago.

他不大可能找到他 40 年前居住过的地方。

3. 限制性和非限制性定语从句

定语从句有限制性和非限制性两种。限制性定语从句是先行词不可缺少的部分，去掉它主句意思往往不明确；非限制性定语从句是先行词的附加说明，去掉了也不会影响主句的意思，它与主句之间通常用逗号分开，但在现代英语中常会碰到不加逗号的情况。例如:

This is the house which we bought last month.

这是我们上个月买的那幢房子。(限制性)

The house, which we bought last month, is very nice.

这幢房子很漂亮,是我们上个月买的。(非限制性)

My house, which I bought last year, has got a lovely garden.

我去年买的那幢房子带着个漂亮的花园。(非限制性)

He seems not to have grasped what I meant, which greatly upsets me.

他似乎没明白我的意思,这使我心烦。(非限制性)

说明:关系代词 that 和关系副词 why 不能引导非限制性定语从句。

Exercises

I. Fill in each blank with a proper relative pronoun or relative adverb.

1. No animals can do all the things _____ human beings can do.

2. This is a city _____ environment has been seriously polluted.

3. Can you suggest a time _____ it will be convenient to meet?
4. Is there a shop around _____ we can get food?
5. The summer of 1969, the year _____ men first set foot on the moon, will never be forgotten.
6. He studied hard and later became a well-known writer, _____ was what his father had expected.
7. I still remember the summer _____ we had the big drought.
8. The real estate company from _____ we bought our house is bankrupt.
9. The tiles _____ fell off the roof caused serious damage.
10. A doctor examined the astronauts _____ returned from space today.

II. **Complete each of the following sentences with the most appropriate word or words from the four choices marked A, B, C and D.**

1. The Thames, _____ is now clean enough to swim in, was polluted for over a hundred years.
   A. that   B. which   C. who   D. where
2. The weather turned out fine, _____ was more than we could expect.
   A. what   B. which   C. that   D. it
3. It was an agreement the details _____ could not be altered.
   A. that   B. which   C. of which   D. on which
4. The person _____ I complain to is the manager.
   A. to whom   B. whom   C. whose   D. which
5. He is the man _____ the pictures were stolen.
   A. whose house   B. from which
   C. from whose house   D. from whom
6. He often thinks of the days _____ he spent abroad.
   A. when   B. on which   C. that   D. in which
7. The Tower of London, _____ so many people lost their lives, is now a tourist attraction.
   A. which   B. where   C. that   D. there
8. The building _____ windows we can see from here is a primary school.
   A. who   B. which   C. whose   D. that

9. The reason _____ Asian elephants are easily trained is _____ they have good memories.

   A. why... that   B. what... that   C. that... that   D. why... what

10. Of all the books he writes, it is the only one _____ I dislike.

    A. which   B. of which   C. what   D. that

Part III Reading Practice

Guide to Reading

1. Words and Expressions to Learn

length	n.	长度
admire	v.	钦佩；赞赏；羡慕
unaware	adj.	未意识到的，不知道的
confident	adj.	自信的
courage	n.	勇气，胆量
possibility	n.	可能；可能性
modify	v.	变更，修改
aid	n&v.	帮助，救助
set about one's work		开始工作
stare at		凝视，盯着看
come up with		提出，拿出
single out		挑选
end up		结束；死
due to		由于，应归于
in horror		震惊地；恐怖地

2. Pre-Reading Questions

(1) What was your dream in your childhood?
(2) Do you think your dream will come true?

Young Flyers

1   When I was younger my imagination was one that wasn't **grounded** (*v.* 基于) by physics or any real **common sense** (*n.* 常识). It was caught up in Peter Pan and the Loch Ness **monster** (*n.* 妖怪) and I believed it... so did my two brothers: Brad my twin, and John who is two years older than me.

2   When I was seven I **became fixated on** (集中在……上) birds, wondering what it would be like to fly like that, and decided to **bypass** (*v.* 绕开) primary, high school and university education and become an **aeronautical** (*adj.* 航空学的) engineer. I wanted to make an aeroplane (or a **glider** (*n.* 滑翔机) at least) to set my imagination free—but it couldn't be done without a team, so I enlisted my brothers. I knew them: we all wanted to fly like all kids who hadn't met reality.

3   We were excited, and set about our task. It would need careful planning. We got three **planks** (*n.* 厚木板) of tongue and **groove** (*n.* 凹槽) pine from the timber pile at the back of the shed, and cut one into a short length, another into a medium length, and another into a long length. We nailed the short piece at one end of the long piece, and the medium piece about a quarter from the other end. We stood back to admire our masterpiece. A **two-dimensional** (*adj.* 两维的) shape of an airplane lay on the shed floor. We had done it!

4   My twin brother sat on it with joy: "Look guys. I'm flying! I'm flying!" He looked like a **rodeo** (*n.* 牛仔竞技表演) cowboy whipping his horse—unaware it was dead. "Okay, let's fly this **puppy** (*n.* 小家伙)," John said. So we dragged the two-metre length of wood up the tree next to the shed, and placed it in position to be pushed off the roof with somebody on it. "So who's going on it?" John said. We stared at each other. Then we took a long look down at the ground below. "You should go, Scott; you came up with the idea." John said. I looked at the plane. My imagination had run away. It didn't look like the plane I'd imagined at all, just planks of wood laid on one another. "John, Mum always says you're the oldest so you should make a good example of yourself. So you should go first," I said. (This very excuse earned John a lot of scars over the years.) "Yeah!" Brad said, confident in my argument, or maybe frightened to be singled out. John took another look at that plank of wood. He looked scared. I was sure he wasn't going to do it,

and we would **end up** (告终) **dumping** (v. 倾卸) it. "Alright," he said finally "but you have to push really hard, okay?" Brad and I nodded, and watched our brave brother **man** (v. 在……就位) the position as pilot and prepare himself. I guess his courage was also due to the fact that there was the strong possibility he would experience flying over into the neighbour's backyard. "Ready?" we asked John. "Yep." "One, two, three... **blastoff** (n. 发射)!" We pushed him off the roof and watched in horror as the plane **instantly** (adv. 立即地) nose-dived and **stabbed** (v. 刺) into the ground. Our brother landed on his feet for a moment before falling on his face—the plane then fell backward onto him. He got up and began **hopping** (v. 单脚跳) carefully on one foot. "Are you alright, John?" I called down to my brother. "I think I've **jarred** (v. 震动) my foot," he shouted. We climbed back down the tree and made sure his foot wasn't broken. The aeroplane would have to be modified, but that was for another day. Brad and I had learned from our brother. We went inside, turned on the TV, and who should we see but Mickey Mouse doing exactly what we had tried to do with only the aid of a **broom stick** (扫帚条子)—we headed for the **closet** (n. 储藏室).

(*647 words*)

 **Exercises**

Reading Comprehension

I. Answer the following questions according to the passage.

1. Why did the author and his brothers produce a plane?
2. How did they make the plane?
3. Why did John have to practice the plan?
4. What was the result of their flight?
5. What did the author learn from his old brother?

II. Translate into Chinese the following sentences taken from the passage.

1. I wanted to make an aeroplane (or a glider at least) to set my imagination free.
2. We were excited, and set about our task.
3. It didn't look like the plane I'd imagined at all, just planks of wood laid on one another.
4. We climbed back down the tree and made sure his foot wasn't broken.
5. Our brother landed on his feet for a moment before falling on his face.

III. Fill in the blanks with the words or phrases listed in Word and Expressions to Learn. Change the form where necessary.

1. He answered the questions with _____.
2. We are fully _____ of the gravity of the situation.
3. Her success _____ me to try the same thing.
4. I'll do everything _____ to help you.
5. His heart sickened at the thought of that _____ scene.
6. The two countries were on the point of war _____ the diplomatic disputes.
7. The little girl _____ the little cats tumbling over each other in their basket.
8. A dictionary is an invaluable _____ in learning a new language.

Part IV   Practical English

Business Correspondences（业务信函）（五）

8. Letters of Application

求职信一般有五个组成部分：写信动机、自我介绍、本人能力、结尾、附件。

写信人应述明自己的年龄或出生年月、教育背景，尤其与应征职位有关的训练或教育科目、工作经验或特殊技能。本人能力的陈述是非常重要的，因为它体现你究竟能为公司做什么，直接关系到求职的成功率。但是也要注意一定要用最少的文字表达最多的意思。在最后应希望并请求未来的雇主允以面谈的机会，因此信中要表明可以面谈的时间。

Sample

Letter of Application

338 E. 44th St. Apt. 11A
New York, NY 10017
U.S.A.
May 16, 2006

Professor Wang Yiming
Department of English
Beijing Foreign Studies University
Beijing, 100081
People's Republic of China

Dear Professor Wang,

　　I am interested in teaching English in the People's Republic of China. I am qualified to teach reading, writing and literature. An acquaintance of mine, Mr. Liu Yongli of your university, suggested that I should write to you.

Presently, I work as a teaching assistant in City College in Los Angeles, California, U.S.A. My background is strong in the liberal arts, especially in the English language. I have a Ph.D. degree in linguistics from University of Michigan.

Enclosed you will find a copy of my resume. Basically, I am interested in a position as a foreign language expert or as a teacher.

If you have any position available, please allow me to interview with you.

Thank you for your time and consideration.

Respectfully yours,
(Signature)
Christine Stein

Encl.

（省略）

尊敬的王易鸣教授：

我想到中国教英语，并能够胜任阅读、写作和文学的教学工作。贵校的刘勇毅先生是我的朋友，他建议我给您写信。

目前我在加利福尼亚洛杉矶的城市大学担任助教工作。在校期间主修文科，尤以英语语言见长。拥有密歇根大学的语言学博士学位。

随信附上我的简历。我个人希望能够得到一个外国语言学专家或是教师的职位。

如果您有适合的职位，请允许我参加面试。

非常感谢。

充满敬意的
（签名）
克瑞斯汀·斯坦恩

9. Self-recommendation

自荐信的书写格式与一般书信相同,信的开始要先做自我介绍,包括姓名、学校、所学专业等。书写内容主要是谈谈自己对从事此工作感兴趣的原因、愿意到该单位工作的愿望和自己具有的资格。最后,要提出你希望能有面试的机会,附联系地址、邮政编码、电话。

Sample

Sichuan Publishing House
78 People Street, Jinjiang District
Chengdu, 610000, P. R. of China
July 15, 2006

P.O. Box 690
New York, N.Y.10019
U.S.A

Dear Sir,

  I wish to apply for a position with your publishing house. I'm 31 years old and am at present employed by Sichuan Publishing House, where I have been for the past five years. Formerly I was employed by Education Press where I was nearly three years.

  My only reason for leaving either of those positions would be to better myself and I feel there is no further opportunity in my present position.

  The editorial work has always had a great appeal to me as I have some ability in writing and editorial work.

  I can give you references from both these press houses as to my character and ability as an editor.

Very truly yours,
(Signature)
Wang Fang

> (省略)
>
> 尊敬的先生：
>
>   我希望能在贵社谋求一个职位。我现年 31 岁。目前受雇于四川出版社，最近 5 年本人一直在该社工作。在这之前，本人还在教育出版社工作将近 3 年。
>
>   我打算离开这两个职位的唯一理由就是谋求高升。我觉得目前的职位不利于本人的发展。
>
>   由于我在写作和编辑工作方面有些能力，所以编辑工作一直对我有很大的吸引力。
>
>   关于我的人品和能力，我可以请上述两个出版单位写介绍信以供参考。
>
> 真诚的
（签名）
王　方

常用套语：

1. I am writing to you in the hope of obtaining a teaching position in your department.

   我写信来是希望能够在贵系获得一个教师的职位。

2. I would like to apply for the position of proofreader which you advertised in June 16 issue of *Beijing Youth*.

   我希望申请你们在 6 月 16 日《北京青年报》上招聘的校对的工作。

3. Enclosed please find three letters of recommendation and my resume.

   随信附上我的简历和三封推荐信。

4. I am available for an interview every afternoon except Wednesday.

   除了星期三，我每天下午都有时间接受你们的面试。

5. Thank you for your consideration. I look forward very much to hearing from you soon.

   非常感谢，我期待着收到你的回信。

6. In reply to your advertisement in today's newspaper, I respectfully offer my services for the situation.

   拜读今日报纸上贵公司广告，本人特此备函应征该职位。

7. Learning from Mr. S.P. Chen that you are looking for a sales manager, I should like to apply for the position.

   从陈少朋先生处得悉，贵公司正在招聘一名业务经理，我愿应招此职。

8. I have been for over five years in the employ of an exporting company.

本人曾经有五年多受雇于一家出口贸易公司。

Writing Practice

Complete the following letter according to the Chinese version.

> 尊敬的人事部经理：
> 　　本人需要一份工作,不是任何公司的任何工作,而是贵公司的一个职位。贵公司不只是商店,而是大众都知晓的机构。无论是对员工还是对客户,它的公正、诚实的美誉远近驰名。
> 　　在大学主修会计四年来,我早就想到贵公司会计部工作,今年七月即将毕业。写此信时,不知贵公司目前是否有空缺,但是下列的资历促使本人冒昧提出申请。
> 　　（略）
>
> 　　　　　　　　　　　　宁红大学会计学院
> 　　　　　　　　　　　　　　（签名）
> 　　　　　　　　　　　　　　张元明

Attention of Personnel Manager,

　　I want a job. Not any job with any company, but a ＿＿＿ (1) job with your company. Here are my reasons. Your organization is more ＿＿＿ (2) just a business house. It is an institution in the minds of the local public. It has a ＿＿＿ (3) for fair play and honesty with both employees and customers alike.

　　For the past four years, while ＿＿＿ (4) in accounting at college, I have had a secret ambition to work for your organization in the ＿＿＿ (5) department. I'll graduate in July. As I write this letter, I am wondering if there is an opening at present, but here are my qualifications which prompt me to ＿＿＿ (6) an application now.

　　(Omitted)

　　　　　　　　　　　　　　　　Yours faithfully,
　　　　　　　　　　　　　　　　　(Signature)
　　　　　　　　　　　　　　　　Zhang Yuanming
　　　　　　　　　　Accounting School, Ninghong University

Part V English Salon

Funny Questions

1. What goes all over the house, but touches nothing?
2. Why is the letter "t" like an island?
3. Why do you think B comes before C?
4. My uncle has a brother, he is not my uncle. Who is he?
5. Why is autumn the best time for a lazy person to read a book?
6. Why did the boy take a ladder to school?
7. Two Japanese are standing on a hill. One is the father of the other's son. What's the relationship between the two Japanese?

 Requirement

Try to find out the answers to these questions.

Vocabulary

符号说明：达到《高职高专教育英语课程教学基本要求》B 级应掌握的词汇：★
达到《高职高专教育英语课程教学基本要求》A 级应掌握的词汇：▲
大学英语 4~6 级词汇：♨

♨ abnormal	/æb'nɔːməl/	adj.	not typical, usual, or regular; not normal 反常的,变态的,不正常的	Unit 4
♨ academic	/ˌækə'demik/	adj.	relating to scholarly performance 有关学术的	Unit 1
★ accent	/'æksənt/	v.	put emphasis on 强调,使显著	Unit 5
★ achieve	/ə'tʃiːv/	v.	succeed in doing 成功完成	Unit 8
▲ alter	/'ɔːltə/	v.	become different; to make sth/sb different (使)变动,更改	Unit 8
♨ angle	/'æŋgl/	n.	the figure formed by two lines diverging from a common point; the place, position, or direction from which an object is presented to view [数]角;视角	Unit 7
▲ appearance	/ə'piərəns/	n.	what sb or sth appears to be; the thing which shows 外表,外貌,外观	Unit 4
▲ appetite	/'æpitait/	n.	desire, esp. for food	

207

			胃口；食欲	Unit 6
★ appreciate	/əˈpriːʃieit/	v.	judge rightly the value of; understand and enjoy	
			正确地判断……的价值；鉴赏；重视	Unit 4
▲ artificial	/ɑːtiˈfiʃəl/	adj.	made by humans; lacking true	
			人(工)造的	Unit 6
▲ associate	/əˈsəuʃieit/	v.	connect or join together; combine	
			使发生联系，联合	Unit 7
★ assure	/əˈʃuə/	v.	cause to feel sure	
			使确信	Unit 1
♨ astounding	/əˈstaundiŋ/	adj.	amazing	
			令人惊奇的	Unit 6
★ attach	/əˈtætʃ/	v.	fasten; cause to join	
			依附	Unit 6
★ available	/əˈveiləbl/	adj.	present and ready for use; accessible; obtainable	
			可用的；可获得的，可得到的	Unit 2
♨ awareness	/əˈweənis/	n.	having realization of sth, be conscious of sth	
			意识	Unit 3

B

★ basis	/ˈbeisis/	n.	a foundation upon which sth rests	
			基础	Unit 7
♨ beneficiary	/ˌbeniˈfiʃəri/	n.	a person who receives sth or who benefits from sth	
			受益者，受惠者	Unit 3
▲ budget	/ˈbʌdʒit/	n.	a sum of money allocated for a particular purpose	
			预算	Unit 2

| ★ button | /'bʌtn/ | n. | a switch on a machine 按钮 | Unit 6 |

C

★ candidate	/'kændidit/	n.	a person taking an examination 应试者	Unit 1
♨ capability	/ˌkeipə'biliti/	n.	the quality of being capable 能力	Unit 6
★ career	/kə'riə/	n.	the general course of one's working life 生涯,经历	Unit 1
♨ carefree	/'kɛəfriː/	adj.	without responsibilities or worries; cheerful 无忧无虑的,快乐的	Unit 4
★ challenge	/tʃælindʒ/	n.&v.	(a) call to engage in a contest, fight, or competition 挑战	Unit 2
♨ chill	/tʃil/	n.	coldness; feeling of gloom and depression 寒冷；(心情)冰冷,阴沉	Unit 3
▲ circuit	/'səːkit/	n.	circular path of an electric current 电路	Unit 6
▲ combination	/ˌkɔmbi'neiʃən/	n.	the act of combining or the state of being combined 联合,合并	Unit 7
★ comfort	/'kʌmfət/	n.	consolation (for loss, etc.); sb or sth that brings consolation 安慰,抚慰	Unit 5
★ compare	/kəm'pɛə/	v.	examine people or things to see how they are alike and how they are different 比较	Unit 6

♨ compassion	/kəm'pæʃən/	n.	pity; feeling for the sufferings of others, prompting one to give help 同情,怜悯 Unit 4
▲ component	/kəm'pəunənt/	n.	any of the parts of which sth is made 组件,部件 Unit 6
♨ computational	/ˌkɔmpju(:)'teiʃ(ə)n(ə)l/	adj.	of calculation 计算方面的;使用计算机的 Unit 6
★ confidence	/'kɔnfidəns/	n.	belief in oneself or others 信心,信任 Unit 4
▲ confront	/kən'frʌnt/	v.	face 面对,面临 Unit 3
♨ connection	/kə'nekʃən/	n.	being connected 连接 Unit 6
♨ consciousness	/'kɔnʃəsnis/	n.	all the ideas, feelings, opinions held by a person 意识 Unit 6
★ cope	/kəup/	v.	(with "with") to deal with a situation, problem (同 with 连用)对付,处理,解决 Unit 5
★ costly	/'kɔstli/	adj.	expensive 昂贵的 Unit 1
★ crisis (*pl.* crises)	/'kraisis/	n.	turning point in illness, life, history; time of difficulty 转机;危机 Unit 5
▲ crucial	/'kru:ʃəl/	adj.	decisive; critical; fundamental 有决定性的;极重要的;根本的 Unit 5

| ★ cure | /kjuə/ | v. | (sb or sth) make a person or animal healthy again after an illness 治愈 Unit 8 |

D

ꙮ decline	/dɪˈklaɪn/	v.	decrease 下降 Unit 8
ꙮ deficient	/dɪˈfɪʃənt/	adj.	incomplete, inadequate 不完全的；不完美的；不充足的 Unit 3
★ define	/dɪˈfaɪn/	v.	state the precise meaning of (a word or sense of a word, for example); describe the nature or basic qualities of; explain 给……下定义；描述，解释 Unit 7
★ delicate	/ˈdelɪkɪt/	adj.	tender; fine; easily broken or injured 精致的；易破的 Unit 6
ꙮ dental	/ˈdentl/	adj.	of, relating to, or intended for dentistry 牙科的 Unit 1
★ detail	/ˈdiːteɪl/	n.	an individual part or item 细目，细节 Unit 2
ꙮ diet	/ˈdaɪət/	n.	food and drink usually taken 饮食；食物 Unit 6
ꙮ discriminative	/dɪsˈkrɪmɪnətɪv/	adj.	being biased against sth 不公平的，歧视的 Unit 3
ꙮ disdain	/dɪsˈdeɪn/	n.	a feeling or show of contempt and aloofness; scorn 轻视，蔑视 Unit 4
▲ distort	/dɪsˈtɔːt/	v.	pull or twist sth out of its usual shape; misrepresent 使(某物)变形，扭曲；曲解 Unit 4

211

divinity	/di'viniti/	n.	theology 神学	Unit 1
dormitory	/'dɔːmitri/	n.	a building for housing a number of persons, as at a school 宿舍	Unit 1
drama	/'drɑːmə/	n.	theatrical plays of a particular kind or period 戏剧	Unit 1
dumb	/dʌm/	adj.	incapable of using speech 哑的	Unit 2

E

efficient	/i'fiʃənt/	adj.	having efficiency 高效的	Unit 8
elevate	/'eliveit/	v.	move (sth) to a higher place or position from a lower one; lift 提高,提升	Unit 7
eliminate	/i'limineit/	v.	get rid of; remove 消灭;消除	Unit 7
embarrassing	/im'bærəsiŋ/	adj.	making sb feel awkward or ashamed 令人困窘的,令人难堪的	Unit 4
emerge	/i'məːdʒ/	v.	come out of a dark, enclosed or hidden place (从暗处)出现	Unit 8
enable	/i'neibl/	v.	make it possible for someone to do something, or for something to happen 使能够	Unit 2
encounter	/in'kauntə/	v.	meet, especially unexpectedly; come upon 不期而遇,偶然遇见	Unit 4

♨ encouragement	/inˈkʌridʒmənt/	n.	action of encouraging ; thing that encourages 鼓励,支持,激励,促进(的事物)	Unit 4
♨ enrollment	/inˈrəulmənt/	v.	the act or process of enrolling 注册,登记	Unit 1
♨ erode	/iˈrəud/	v.	wear away; eat into 腐蚀;侵蚀	Unit 5
★ essential	/iˈsenʃəl/	adj.	basic or indispensable; necessary 基本的,必须的	Unit 1
▲ exceed	/ikˈsiːd/	v.	be greater than; do more than 超过	Unit 6
▲ excessive	/ikˈsesiv/	adj.	greater than what seems reasonable or appropriate 过度的,过分的	Unit 8
★ experience	/iksˈpiəriəns/	v.	undergo; feel 经历;体验;具有	Unit 6
★ extent	/iksˈtent/	n.	how large, important, or serious something is, etc. 范围;程度	Unit 2
★ external	/eksˈtəːnl/	adj.	on, of, or for the outside 外部的;外面的	Unit 6
▲ extraordinary	/iksˈtrɔːdnri/	adj.	beyond what is usual 非凡的;惊人的	Unit 6

F

★ facility	/fəˈsiliti/	n.	sth created to serve a particular function 设备	Unit 1
▲ faculty	/ˈfækəlti/	n.	a body of teachers 全体教师	Unit 1

★ favorable	/ˈfeivərəbl/	adj.	helpful, suitable, good 有帮助的,合适的,良好的	Unit 3
♨ feat	/fiːt/	n.	difficult action successfully done 伟绩;功绩	Unit 6
♨ formulate	/ˈfɔːmjuleit/	v.	create sth in a precise form, make 使形式固定,制定	Unit 3
★ fortune	/ˈfɔːtʃən/	n.	wealth 大量财产;财富	Unit 1
♨ fragile	/ˈfrædʒail/	adj.	easily broken or damaged 易碎的	Unit 6
★ function	/ˈfʌŋkʃən/	v.	operate; act 运行;发挥作用	Unit 5

G

★ gap	/ˈgæp/	n.	opening or break in sth 间隙;缺口,裂口	Unit 6
♨ generate	/ˈdʒenəˌreit/	v.	produce; cause sth to occur 生成;产生	Unit 6
★ generation	/ˌdʒenəˈreiʃən/	n.	single stage in a family history (家史中的)一代	Unit 4
♨ goof	/ˈguːf/	n.	an incompetent, foolish, or stupid person 傻瓜,笨蛋	Unit 2
♨ grass-roots	/ˈgrɑːsˈruːts/	n.	ordinary people 平民,群众,基层	Unit 3

H

| ♨ heritage | /ˈheritidʒ/ | n. | something that is passed down from preceding generations 遗产;传统 | Unit 1 |
| ★ horizon | /həˈraizn/ | n. | line where the sky seems to meet the earth or sea 地平线 | Unit 6 |

| ♨ hug | /hʌg/ | n. | the act of putting the arms round tightly, esp. to show love 拥抱 | Unit 5 |
| ♨ hum | /hʌm/ | v. | buzz; sing with closed lips 发嗡嗡声 | Unit 6 |

★ ideal	/ai'diəl/	adj.	the best or most suitable that something could possibly be 理想的	Unit 2
★ identify	/ai'dentifai/	v.	say, show, prove who or what sb or sth is 使等同于；验明	Unit 5
▲ illustrate	/'iləstrieit/	v.	clarify, as by use of examples or comparisons 说明	Unit 1
♨ indifference	/in'difrəns/	n.	a lack of interest, feeling or reaction toward sb/sth 漠不关心，冷淡	Unit 8
▲ individual	/ˌindi'vidjuəl/	adj.	single; separate 个别的；单个的，个人的	Unit 6
▲ inevitable	/in'evitəbl/	adj.	unavoidable; certain to happen 不可避免的，一定会发生的	Unit 5
▲ infect	/in'fekt/	v.	cause sb or sth to have a disease 传染，使受感染	Unit 6
♨ inhabitant	/in'hæbitənt/	n.	a person or animal living in a particular place 居民；栖息动物	Unit 8
▲ insight	/'insait/	n.	understanding; power of seeing into sth with the mind 洞察力，眼光	Unit 5

215

▲ institution	/ˌinstiˈtjuːʃn/	n.	an established organization or foundation, especially one dedicated to education, public service, or culture (教育或文化)机构 Unit 1
▲ intelligence	/inˈtelidʒəns/	n.	capacity to acquire and apply knowledge 才智；学习和应用知识的能力 Unit 4
★ internal	/inˈtɜːnl/	adj.	of or on the inside 内部的；里面的 Unit 6
▲ investigate	/inˈvestigeit/	v.	inquire carefully about 调查；了解 Unit 6
▲ investment	/inˈvestmənt/	n.	the act of investing, esp. of money 投资 Unit 5
★ invitation	/ˌinviˈteiʃn/	n.	thing that tempts or encourages sb to do sth 鼓励，激励；引诱的事物 Unit 4
★ involve	/inˈvɔlv/	v.	be affected by or taken part in 牵涉；参加 Unit 8

| journalism | /ˈdʒɜːnlizəm/ | n. | collecting, writing, editing, and presentation of news or news articles in newspapers and magazines and in radio and television broadcasts 新闻报道 Unit 1 |

| know-how | /nəu-hau/ | n. | practical knowledge or skill in an activity 实践知识或技术；本事；技能 Unit 3 |

♨ laid-off	/leɔd-if/	adj.	dismissed from the work 下岗	Unit 3
▲ launch	/lɔːntʃ/	v.	set going; initiate 发动；开始	Unit 1
▲ leap	/'liːp/	n.	jump; rapid change or increase 跳；激增；骤变	Unit 3
★ leisure	/'liːʒə/	n.	freedom from time-consuming duties, responsibilities, or activities 空闲，闲暇	Unit 2
★ level	/'levəl/	n.	a degree of attainment 水平；(一定)的标准	Unit 6
★ likely	/'laikli/	adj.&adv.	probable; probably 很可能(的)；大概；多半	Unit 6
♨ literally	/'litərəli/	adv.	without exaggeration; strictly, word for word 实在地；完全地	Unit 5
♨ lure	/ljuə/	v.	attract or attempt sb 吸引，诱惑	Unit 3

▲ maintain	/mein'tein/	v.	keep up or carry on; continue 维持或保持；继续	Unit 7
★ mass	/'mæs/	n.	a large solid lump or pile 团；块	Unit 6
★ metal	/'metl/	n.	a hard, usually shiny substance used to make machines. etc. 金属的	Unit 6

217

mentality	/menˈtæliti/	n.	characteristic attitude of mind; way of thinking
			心态，精神状态 Unit 3
★ mention	/ˈmenʃən/	v.	speak or write sth about; say the name of; refer to
			提起；叙述 Unit 5
▲ minority	/maiˈnɔriti/	n.	a racial, religious, political, national, or other group regarded as different from the larger group of which it is part
			少数 Unit 1
misfortune	/misˈfɔːtʃən/	n.	bad luck; unfortunate condition, accident or event
			不幸，灾祸，不幸事故 Unit 4
molecule	/ˈmɔlikjuːl/	n.	the smallest unit into which any substance can be divided without losing its own chemical nature
			（化学）分子 Unit 6

★ neglect	/niˈglekt/	v.	pay too little attention to something
			忽视，疏忽 Unit 2
nerd	/nəːd/	n.	a person regarded as stupid, inept, or unattractive
			蠢货 Unit 2
neurological	/njuərəuˈlɔdʒikəl/	adj.	of scientific study of nerves and their diseases
			神经学（上）的 Unit 6
▲ numerous	/ˈnjuːmərəs/	adj.	(formal) existing in large numbers
			许多的 Unit 8

O

obstacle	/ˈɔbstəkl/	n.	thing in the way that either stops or makes it difficult 障碍, 妨碍物 Unit 3
★ otherwise	/ˈʌðəwaiz/	adv.	in another or different way 在其他方面; 以另外的方式 Unit 5
★ outstanding	/autˈstændiŋ/	adj.	excellent, extremely good 杰出的, 优秀的 Unit 8
▲ overload	/ˈəuvəˈləud/	v.	load too heavily 使超载, 使过载 Unit 7

P

plug	/ˈplʌg/	v.	insert sth into 接上插头通电 Unit 6
▲ pose	/pəuz/	v.	raise a question (esp. one that needs serious thought) 提问, 质询 Unit 8
▲ potential	/pəˈtenʃ(ə)l/	adj.	capable of being but not yet in existence 潜在的, 可能的
		n.	inherent ability or capacity for growth, development, or coming into being 潜力 Unit 2
★ principal	/ˈprinsəpəl/	adj.	chief 重要的, 首要的 Unit 1
productivity	/ˌprɔdʌkˈtiviti/	n.	ability to produce; productive yield 生产(率) Unit 5

▲ promote	/prəˈməut/	v.	contribute to the progress or growth of 促进，推进 Unit 7
★ proper	/ˈprɔpə/	adj.	right; suitable 合适的；恰当的 Unit 6
▲ pursue	/pəˈsjuː/	v.	follow in an effort to overtake or capture; chase 为了赶上或捕获而努力跟随；追求 Unit 2

R

▲ rank	/ræŋk/	n.	a relative position or degree of value in a graded group 顺序，次序 Unit 1
♨ recruit	/riˈkruːt/	v.	gain sb as new member 吸收某人为新成员，招募 Unit 3
♨ recycle	/ˌriːˈsaikl/	v.	treat things been used so that they can be used again 回收利用 Unit 8
♨ regeneration	/riˌdʒenəˈreiʃən/	n.	being given new life or vigor to 新生；再生 Unit 5
▲ release	/riˈliːs/	v.	set free 释放 Unit 6
★ renew	/riˈnjuː/	v.	make new again or as if new; revive, reawaken 恢复；更新；变新 Unit 5
★ response	/risˈpɔns/	n.	a reaction, as that of an organism or a mechanism, to a specific stimulus 反应 Unit 2
★ resume	/ˈrezjuːmei/	n.	brief account of sb's previous career, usu. submitted with an application for a job 个人简历，履历 Unit 3

★ robot	/ˈrəubɔt/	n.	a computer controlled machine which can move and do some of the work of a human being	
			机器人	Unit 6
♨ rot	/rɔt/	v.	decay or become useless	
			腐烂；枯朽	Unit 5
▲ routine	/ruːˈtiːn/	n.	a prescribed, detailed course of action to be followed regularly; a standard procedure	
			例行公事；常规；日常事务；程序	Unit 7

♨ saturate	/ˈsætʃəreit/	v.	make sth wet; fill sb/sth completely with sth	
			浸湿；充满某物	Unit 3
▲ severe	/siˈviə/	adj.	very bad, intense, difficult	
			非常恶劣、紧张、困难	Unit 3
★ shift	/ʃift/	v.	change from one position or direction to another	
			改变位置或方向	Unit 3
♨ sightless	/ˈsaitlis/	adj.	unable to see; blind	
			看不见的，失明的	Unit 4
★ signal	/ˈsignl/	n.	a sound or action to warn, command or give message	
			信号	Unit 6
♨ significantly	/sigˈnifikəntli/	adv.	in a way that is large or important enough to have an effect on sth	
			有重大意义地，显著地	Unit 8
♨ similarity	/ˌsimiˈlæriti/	n.	being similar; likeness; similar feature or aspect	
			相似(性)	Unit 6

▲ snack	/snæk/	v.	have a very slight, hurried meal 吃快餐 Unit 5
★ special	/'speʃəl/	adj.	not ordinary or usual; of a particular kind 特别的;专门的 Unit 6
♨ specialty	/'speʃlti/	n.	interest, activity, subject, etc. in which a person majors 专业;特长 Unit 3
♨ spider	/'spaidə/	n.	any of many kinds of small creatures which make silk threads into nets for catching insects to eat 蜘蛛 Unit 6
▲ spirit	/'spirit/	n.	soul; immaterial, intellectual or mental part of man 精神;灵魂 Unit 5
▲ staff	/stɑːf/	n.	the personnel who carry out a specific enterprise 全体雇员 Unit 1
♨ steadily	/'stedili/	adv.	(development, growth) gradually and in an even and regular way (发展、增长等)稳步地,持续地 Unit 8
♨ stitch	/stitʃ/	v.	sew 缝合 Unit 4
★ strengthen	/'streŋθən/	v.	make strong or increase the strength of 加强 Unit 7
★ stroke	/strəuk/	v.	pass the hand gently over a surface, usu. again and again (用手)轻抚(某物表面) Unit 4
♨ subtle	/'sʌtl/	adj.	cunning, clever; difficult to perceive 狡猾的,阴险的;难以察觉的 Unit 5
♨ surge	/sɜːdʒ/	n.	a sudden abnormal rise of current followed by a drop 汹涌;冲动 Unit 6

♨ surplus	/ˈsɜːpləs/	adj.	more than is needed or used 剩余的，过剩的	Unit 3
★ survey	/sɜːˈveɪ/	n.	investigation 调查	Unit 8
♨ susceptible	/səˈseptəbl/	adj.	likely to suffer from 影响或损害	Unit 6
▲ switch	/swɪtʃ/	n.	apparatus for stopping or starting an electronic current 开关；电闸	Unit 6
♨ switchboard	/ˈswɪtʃˌbɔːd/	n.	place where telephone lines in a large building are connected 电话总机	Unit 6

★ tend	/tend/	vt.	be inclined to move; have a direction 倾向，有某种趋势，趋于	Unit 4
★ throat	/θrəʊt/	n.	the front part of the neck, the upper part of the passage leading from mouth to the stomach and lungs 喉	Unit 5
▲ tone	/təʊn/	v.	become stronger, brighter, more effective, etc. 增强	Unit 7
★ total	/ˈtəʊtl/	adj.	complete; whole 总的；总共的	Unit 6
★ transfer	/trænsˈfɜː/	v.	move sth or sb from one place to another; change; move 传递	Unit 6
♨ transplant	/trænsˈplɑːnt/	v.	take an organ from one person and put it into another （器官）移植	Unit 6
▲ trap	/træp/	n.	device for catching animals, etc.;

223

			plan for deceiving sb; trick or device to make sb say or do sth he does not wish to do or say 陷阱；诡计	Unit 5
♨ trillion	/'triljən/	n.&pron.	one million million million 一兆，一万亿	Unit 6

U

★ unlike	/'ʌn'laik/	adj.&prep.	not like; different from 不像(的)；与……不同(的)	Unit 6
▲ utilize	/'juːtilaiz/	v.	make use of 利用	Unit 8

V

▲ vary	/'veəri/	v.	make or cause changes in the characteristics or attributes of; modify or alter; give variety to; make diverse 变更，改变；使变化，使多样化	Unit 7
★ video	/'vidiəu/	n.	visual portion of a televised broadcast; television 映像；电视	Unit 7
▲ visual	/'vizjuəl/	adj.	of or relating to the sense of sight 视力的，视觉的	Unit 1

♨ weedy	/'wiːdi/	adj.	full of plant where it is not desired 杂草丛生的	Unit 5
★ weight	/weit/	n.	a measure of the heaviness of an object	

			重量	Unit 7
★ wisdom	/ˈwizdəm/	n.	quality of being wise	
			智慧	Unit 4
★ within	/wiˈðin/	prep.	inside; not more than	
			在……之内	Unit 6
▲ witness	/ˈwitnis/	v.	be present at sth and see it	
			目击，见证	Unit 3
♨ workout	/ˈwəːkaut/	n.	the activity of exerting your muscles in various ways to keep fit	
			健身；体育锻炼	Unit 7

《Grammar in Context》(4th Edition)

英语语境语法
系列（第四版）

本套书由美国语言教学研究专家特为非英语母语的英语学习者编写的"英语语境语法系列"（分为"1、2、3级，共6册"和"教师参考用书1、2、3册"）。

本系列丛书特点：

将语法点融入有趣的阅读材料，通过对语境主题的不断练习讲授语法，以促进学生的英语学习和认知发展。

包含大量全新的阅读材料，有关美国日常生活的实例，如简历写作、处理远程交易等，有利于学生获得及扩展对美国文化和历史的了解；涵盖所有语法点的清晰的语法图，便于学生快速查阅和掌握语法知识；大量更新的活动设计，讨论、阅读、作文以及创造性思维技巧训练，帮助全面提高学生的语言和交流技能。

我们还提供注解版的教师用书，包含详细的教学要点和建议；教师同时可获赠含大量题库的CD-ROM和教学指导录像，更加方便教师组织测验和教学。

- 英语语境语法 1A / N.艾尔鲍姆·桑德拉 / 32.00
- 英语语境语法 1B / N.艾尔鲍姆·桑德拉 / 32.00
- 英语语境语法 1 教师用书
  　　　　　　/ N.艾尔鲍姆·桑德拉 / 60.00
- 英语语境语法 2A / N.艾尔鲍姆·桑德拉 / 32.00
- 英语语境语法 2B / N.艾尔鲍姆·桑德拉 / 32.00
- 英语语境语法 2 教师用书
  　　　　　　/ N.艾尔鲍姆·桑德拉 / 66.00
- 英语语境语法 3A / N.艾尔鲍姆·桑德拉 / 32.00
- 英语语境语法 3B / N.艾尔鲍姆·桑德拉 / 32.00
- 英语语境语法 3 教师用书
  　　　　　　/ N.艾尔鲍姆·桑德拉 / 68.00

北京大学出版社

外语编辑部电话：010-62767347　　010-62765014
市场营销部电话：010-62750672
邮 购 部 电话：010-62534449